OXFORD WORLD'S CLASSICS

THE COMMUNIST MANIFESTO

KARL MARX (1818–83) was born into a professional family in Trier in the Rhineland. After studying at the University of Berlin, he became a radical journalist, married the aristocratic Jenny von Westphalen, and converted to communism in Paris in 1844. He took an active part in the 1848 revolution in Germany before settling definitively in London, where the family's poverty was partly responsible for the death of three of his six children. His massive studies of political economy issued in *Capital*, the first volume of which was published in 1867, and on which Marx continued to work until his death.

FRIEDRICH ENGELS (1820–95) was born into a prosperous business family in Barmen near Dusseldorf. Although apprenticed to his father's business firm. Engels's sympathies moved quickly in the direction of communism, an orientation which was cemented by the beginning of his lifelong collaboration with Marx in 1844. After the 1848 revolutions, Engels moved to Manchester where he eventually became a partner in his father's firm. On retirement in 1870 he settled in London, from where his books, such as *Anti-Dühring*, had an immense influence on the nascent Marxist movement.

DAVID McLELLAN is Professor of Political Theory at the University of Kent and author of numerous studies of Marx and Marxism. Among his most recent books are *Simone Weil: Utopian Pessimist* and *Unto Caesar: The Political Relevance of Christianity*.

OXFORD WORLD'S CLASSICS

*For over 100 years Oxford World's Classics have brought
readers closer to the world's great literature. Now with over 700
titles—from the 4,000-year-old myths of Mesopotamia to the
twentieth century's greatest novels—the series makes available
lesser-known as well as celebrated writing.*

*The pocket-sized hardbacks of the early years contained
introductions by Virginia Woolf, T. S. Eliot, Graham Greene,
and other literary figures which enriched the experience of reading.
Today the series is recognized for its fine scholarship and
reliability in texts that span world literature, drama and poetry,
religion, philosophy and politics. Each edition includes perceptive
commentary and essential background information to meet the
changing needs of readers.*

OXFORD WORLD'S CLASSICS

====

KARL MARX
AND
FRIEDRICH ENGELS

The Communist Manifesto

====

Edited with an Introduction and Notes by
DAVID McLELLAN

OXFORD
UNIVERSITY PRESS

OXFORD

UNIVERSITY PRESS

Great Clarendon Street, Oxford OX2 6DP

Oxford University Press is a department of the University of Oxford.
It furthers the University's objective of excellence in research, scholarship,
and education by publishing worldwide in

Oxford New York

Athens Auckland Bangkok Bogotá Buenos Aires Calcutta
Cape Town Chennai Dar es Salaam Delhi Florence Hong Kong Istanbul
Karachi Kuala Lumpur Madrid Melbourne Mexico City Mumbai
Nairobi Paris São Paulo Singapore Taipei Tokyo Toronto Warsaw
with associated companies in Berlin Ibadan

Oxford is a registered trade mark of Oxford University Press
in the UK and in certain other countries

Published in the United States
by Oxford University Press Inc., New York

British Library Cataloguing in Publication Data

Data available

Library of Congress Cataloging in Publication Data

Marx, Karl, 1818–1883.
[Manifest der Kommunistichen Partei. English]
The Communist manifesto / Karl Marx and Friedrich Engels; edited
with an introduction by David McLellan.
p. cm.—(Oxford world's classics)
Updated, corrected ed. of the 1888 translation by Samuel Moore.
Includes authors' prefaces written subsequent to the 1848 ed.
1. Communism. I. Engels, Friedrich, 1820–1895. II. Moore,
Samuel. III. McLellan, David. IV. Title. V. Series
HX39.5.A5213 1992 335.42'2—dc20 91–42615

ISBN–13: 978–0–19–283437–9
ISBN–10: 0–19–283437–1

11

Printed in Great Britain by
Clays Ltd, St Ives plc

CONTENTS

INTRODUCTION

Karl Marx and Friedrich Engels were aged 29 and 27 respectively when *The Communist Manifesto* was published in February 1848. They had been close collaborators since 1844, and the *Manifesto* was a condensed and incisive summary of the world-view that they had evolved during their hectic intellectual and political involvement of the previous few years.

When they first met, briefly in 1842, Marx and Engels had not taken to each other. Marx was then trying to make a career as a journalist; originally he had wanted to be a university teacher. Born into a somewhat secularized Jewish family with strong Rabbinic roots, his father was a respected lawyer and encouraged his son's intellectual ambitions. After a year's study in Bonn, the young Marx spent five years at the University of Berlin, still dominated by the philosophy of Hegel who had died a few years previously. Marx joined a group of so-called 'Young Hegelians' which included Bruno Bauer, Ludwig Feuerbach, and Moses Hess, writers who wished to emphasize the dialectical elements of the Master's thought in opposition to its more systematic and conservative aspects. Progress through conflict was the watchword of these anti-establishment radicals, who all had strong interests in religion, philosophy, and politics. Marx completed his doctoral thesis, but when his mentor Bruno Bauer was deprived of his teaching post for unacceptably radical religious views, Marx returned to the more liberal Rhineland and became the editor of its most liberal paper the *Rheinische Zeitung*. When the young Engels called to see the editor of the new paper he was coldly received. Marx saw him as too closely associated with the Young Hegelians, whom Marx was beginning to reject as not sufficiently materialist and realist. Engels lacked the university education of Marx. His father was the owner of a cotton-spinning business and intended his eldest son to succeed him. The young Engels picked up Young Hegelian radicalism while doing military service in Berlin and became a socialist in Manchester, where his father had sent him to work in the English branch of the firm.

While Engels moved to Manchester, Marx went to Paris, then the centre of socialist thought. Here he wrote his *Economic and Philosophical Manuscripts*, the rich outline of a humanistic communism. By now, Marx considered himself to be a communist—whereas 'socialism' tended to be a rather pacific term associated with Utopian schemes, 'communism' was a more militant word, connoting the revolutionary abolition of private property, with echoes of the Parisian Commune of 1793. When Engels met Marx for the second time, on 28 September 1844 at the famous Café de la Régence in Paris, they were immediately attracted to each other and spent the next ten days together: 'Our complete agreement in all theoretical fields became obvious', wrote Engels, 'and our joint work dates from that time.' Marx was soon expelled from Paris for subversive journalism, and settled in Brussels where Engels joined him. In 1845 they set out their views in a work called *The German Ideology*, of which the first section of *The Communist Manifesto* was to be a brief summary. The materialist conception of history contained in this work held that to understand human history it was necessary first of all to understand the material conditions under which people produced their livelihood. Such an understanding revealed the underlying motor of history to be the rise and fall of successive classes as they struggled to retain or conquer control of the all-important productive forces of society. Having found, as they believed, the key to history, Marx and Engels wished to propagate their insights. Marx had written in one of his most famous aphorisms, the Eleventh Thesis on Feuerbach: 'Philosophers have hitherto merely interpreted the world in various ways; the point, however, is to change it.' And a vehicle for changing the world was at hand in the newly formed Communist League.

While writing *The German Ideology* Marx had already been

seeking an outlet for his ideas, and had established a Communist Correspondence Committee which was to be the embryo of all subsequent Communist Internationals. Marx described its aim as 'providing both a discussion of scientific questions and a critical appraisal of popular writings and socialist propaganda that can be conducted in Germany'. As well as linking German socialists with French and British colleagues, a more successful aim of the Committee was to maintain contact with the large groups of German émigré workers, whom the underdeveloped nature of their home economy had encouraged to seek higher living-standards abroad. The largest and best-organized of these colonies was in London, but until the late 1830s their most important centre had been Paris, where exiled German artisans had started in 1836 the League of the Just (a secret society with code-names and passwords), which was itself derived from an earlier League of Outlaws. Its original object was to introduce into Germany the Rights of Man and the Citizen. Very roughly half of its membership came from artisans and half from the professions. The League of the Just participated in the rising organized by Blanqui and Barbès in 1839, and on its failure the majority of its members fled to London where they founded a flourishing branch led by Karl Schapper, a typesetter, Heinrich Bauer, a cobbler, and Joseph Moll, a watchmaker. This in turn created a 'front' organization, the German Workers Educational Union, which had almost a thousand members by the end of 1847 and survived until the First World War.

It was clear to Marx and Engels that the German Communists in London, in terms of numbers and organization, represented by far the most promising entrée for them into working-class politics, particularly because Marx's various European Correspondence Committees never really got off the ground. Although mistrustful of what they saw as the 'intellectual arrogance' of the Brussels Communists, the leaders of the League did feel that their agitational and educational work needed a firmer theoretical foundation. On 20 January 1847 the London Correspondence Committee decided to send Moll (whose views were noticeably closer to Marx's than were Schapper's) to Brussels to solicit the help of Marx and invite him to join the League. Marx and Engels agreed to join on condition that a new programme be worked out which rejected socialism based purely on sentiment, condemned conspiratorial approaches to revolution, and gave the League a more democratic structure.

A Congress to achieve these ends assembled in London in early June 1847, though Marx himself was not present. It did indeed give the League a more democratic constitution, in whose statutes the previous slogan, 'All men are brothers' was replaced by 'Proletarians of all countries—unite'. (Marx was said to have declared that there were many men whose brother he wished on no account to be.) Its name was also changed to the Communist League to emphasize the inappropriateness of the conspiratorial approach. And Engels was left to draft a 'Confession of Faith' to be discussed at a second Congress in the following November.

This time Marx did attend. One of the participants, Frederick Lessner, left a vivid description of the impression he made on this occasion:

Marx was then still a young man, about 28 years old, but he greatly impressed us all. He was of medium height, broad-shouldered, powerful in build, and vigorous in his movements. His forehead was high and finely shaped, his hair thick and pitch-black, his gaze piercing. His mouth already had the sarcastic curl that his opponents feared so much. Marx was a born leader of the people. His speech was brief, convincing and compelling in its logic. He never said a superfluous word; every sentence contained an idea and every idea was an essential link in the chain of his argument. Marx had nothing of the dreamer about him. The more I realised the difference between the Communism of Weitling's time and that of the *Communist Manifesto*, the more clearly I saw that Marx represented the manhood of socialist thought.

According to Engels, Marx 'defended the new theory during fairly lengthy debates. All opposition and doubt was at last overcome and the new principles were unanimously accepted.' The debates lasted a full ten days, during which new statutes were drawn up making it quite clear that the Communist League (although necessarily operating largely in secret) was to have a democratic structure ultimately dependent on an annual Congress, and have as its principle purpose the propagation of publicly declared doctrines. The statutes adopted in June, with their somewhat utopian notions of 'community of goods', were set aside and aims of the League were proclaimed as 'the overthrow of the bourgeoisie, the domination of the proletariat, the abolition of the old bourgeois society based on class antagonisms, and the establishment of a new society without classes and without private property'. At the end of the Congress Marx and Engels were given the task of writing a manifesto to publicize the doctrines of the League.

During December 1847 and January 1848, Marx worked on the *Manifesto* in Brussels. The London Communists had supplied him with a file containing at least three tentative drafts: Engels had composed a short 'confession of faith' incorporating the conclusions at the June Congress and destined for discussion among sections of the League; Moses Hess had proposed an alternative version, described ironically by Engels as 'divinely inspired', which differed from Engels's in appealing to supposedly eternal moral principles in advocating an immediate proletarian revolution; and in October Engels had written a longer draft, entitled 'Principles of Communism' but still in the catechetical form, with twenty-five questions and answers. Engels wrote to Marx about this draft before the two of them left for the second Congress in November:

Think over the Confession of Faith a bit. I think it would be better to drop the catechistic form and call the thing a Communist Manifesto. As a certain amount of history will have to be brought in, I think the present form is unsuitable. I am bringing along what I have done here. It is in a simple narrative form, but miserably edited and done in a terrible hurry.

Marx borrowed quite heavily from Engels's work. In places, however, there is a noticeable difference between the

optimistic, determinist approach of Engels which stemmed from
the Enlightenment and his experiences in industrial England, and
the greater emphasis given by Marx to politics in the light of the
experiences of the French working class. Engels said later that the
Manifesto was 'essentially Marx's work' and that 'the basic thought
... belongs solely and exclusively to Marx'. Thus, notwithstand-
ing the appearance of their two names on the title-page and the
persistent assumption about joint-authorship, the actual drafting
of *The Communist Manifesto* was done exclusively by Marx.

The work almost did not appear at all. Marx always had difficulty in meeting deadlines, and the London communists had to
send him a kind of ultimatum stating that 'if the *Manifesto* does
not arrive in London before Tuesday the 1st of February, further
measures will be taken'. Marx just about managed to comply
with the deadline (the last section is clearly foreshortened and
written in haste) and *The Manifesto of the Communist Party* was
printed in London in mid-February.

The *Manifesto* is very much of its own time. Engels rightly said of
Marx's work that it was based on a combination of German
idealist philosophy, French socialist thought, and British classical
economics. Marx's massive critical studies of Smith and Ricardo
were to come after 1848, when he had definitively moved to
London, and although the *Manifesto* certainly has a firm view of
the economic foundations of social conflict, the framework is
provided by a potent mixture of Hegel with the French revolutionary tradition. While Hegel saw history as the rise and fall of
conflicting cultures, Marx tied these cultures more specifically to
social classes and saw the growing industrial working class as the
key to the revolutionary transformation of society. Europe was
awash with revolutionary expectations during the 1840s, with
Chartist agitation in Britain, a plethora of socialist schemes in
Paris, and fervent preaching of immediate communism among
the German workers. The *Manifesto* was designed to give
authoritative shape and direction to these inchoate and often
inarticulate aspirations.

Marx and Engels divide their work into four sections. The first summarizes the more political aspects of the materialist conception of history set out in *The German Ideology*, and depicts history as driven forward by the constant conflict between those who control the forces of production and those who do not. Extrapolating imaginatively on current conditions, Marx and Engels declare that the present age is unique in that class antagonisms become so polarized that there are two hostile camps facing each other: bourgeoisie and proletariat. They then deliver a striking paean of praise to the revolutionary nature of the bourgeoisie, who had expanded the productive forces enormously and created a world market. (This vision of capitalism as a world process only seems to be finally coming about as a result of the revolutions in Eastern Europe and the breakup of the Soviet Union.) Fresh expansion of these forces, however, had brought about ever-deepening cyclical crises which forced the bourgeoisie periodically to destroy large parts of the productive forces and desperately search for decreasingly available new markets. In so doing, they had also created their own executioners in the proletariat, whose revolutionary consciousness was increased by the dual tendency to class polarization, as the lower middle class and peasantry were forced down into the proletariat, and to impoverishment as competition between capitalists led to cuts in wages. As the self-conscious movement of the immense majority in the interests of the immense majority, the victory of the proletariat was inevitable. Marx and Engels, it will be noted, shared the evolutionary optimism common to many nineteenth-century progressives. Their faith in the salutary effects of the growth of the productive forces was the same as that of the exponents of liberal capitalism: where they differed, of course, was in their view of the nature of these effects.

In the second section Marx and Engels explained that the communists were not opposed to other working-class parties; their interests were those of the proletariat as a whole. Two factors, however, distinguished them from other working-class groups: they were international, and they understood the significance of the proletarian movement. Communist ideas were not invented or discovered, they merely expressed actual relations springing from an existing class-struggle, and could be summed up in a single aim: the abolition of private property. Marx and Engels then deal with four common objections to communism. To the objection that communism deprived people of the right of acquiring property as a fruit of their own labour they reply that, as the property of the petty artisan and small farmer was being abolished anyway by the power of capital, the proletariat did not *have* any property; and capital, being a collective product and the result of the united action of all members of society, should be owned collectively. To the criticism that communists wished to abolish the family and introduce community of women, Marx and Engels reply that communists wished to abolish the bourgeois version of the family—whose very existence was dependent on the absence of family life among the proletariat and on public prostitution. Communists, by contrast, wished to do away with the status of women as mere instruments of production. It was also said that communists wished to abolish countries and nationality. But the working man had no country. Modern industry was abolishing national differences and, with the disappearance of class-antagonisms, hostility between nations would also end. In conclusion, in a section very largely inspired by Engels's draft, there follows a ten-point programme which would be 'generally applicable' in 'the most advanced countries'. It is remarkable for its comparatively tentative and moderate nature. With an eye to an alliance with sections of the bourgeoisie, reform proposals are limited to circulating capital, while production, for the time being, is to remain largely in private hands.

The third section of the *Manifesto* is designed to mark out a distinctive doctrinal position for the Communist League by ruthlessly exposing the deficiencies of rival types of socialism— the reactionary, the bourgeois, and the utopian. Reactionary socialism is represented by the feudal socialism promoted by the aristocracy, the Christian socialism which was merely 'the holy

water with which the priest consecrates the heart-burnings of
the aristocrat', the 'petty-bourgeois' socialism of Sismondi, who
wished to restore corporate guilds in manufacture and patriarchal
relations in agriculture, and finally (and most importantly, since
they were the main rivals of the Communist League) the German or 'true' socialists who, following the philosophy of Feuerbach, appealed to metaphysical notions of alienation and human
nature to found their ineffectual politics. As for the bourgeois
socialism of writers such as Proudhon, Marx and Engels consider
that it only addressed social grievances in order the better to
preserve bourgeois society. The third and last type of socialism
discussed is the Utopian school represented by such men as
Fourier, Saint-Simon, and Owen. These writers had perceived
class-antagonisms, but in their time the proletariat was still in-
sufficiently developed to be a credible force for social change.
Hence they wished to attain their ends by peaceful means and
small-scale experiments, rejecting political—and in particular
revolutionary—action. Since they attacked every principle of
existing society their works were full of insights valuable to the
enlightenment of the working class, but as the modern class-
struggle gathered strength, these Utopian solutions had lost all
practical value or theoretical justification, and their contem-
porary followers were reactionary rather than revolutionary. It is
interesting that, given the theoretical and practical difficulties
that were later seen to be inherent in the socialism of the *Manifesto*, recent years have seen the emergence of more tentative and
pluralist socialisms, often harking back to those that Marx and
Engels criticized so mordantly.

In the fourth and last section of the *Manifesto*, which bears all
the signs of hasty composition under pressure from the deadline
set by the London communists, Marx and Engels deal with the
attitude of communists to various opposition parties: in France
they supported the Social Democrats, in Switzerland the
Radicals, in Poland the Peasant Revolutionaries, in Germany
the bourgeoisie. In particular, they predict in Germany an
imminent bourgeois revolution to be followed immediately by a

proletarian revolution. This timetable may seem surprising given the clearly expressed view of Marx and Engels that history moved in determined stages and that the conditions for socialism had to mature within bourgeois society. But it should be remembered that the leaders of the Communist League tended to be artisans whom the industrial revolution was depriving of a livelihood and who wished, therefore, to see capitalism disappear as soon as possible.

For all the clarity and force which later made it a classic, the publication of the *Communist Manifesto* went virtually unnoticed. No sooner was it off the press than the European-wide revolutions of 1848 began. Marx moved back to Germany, where he became the editor of a radical-liberal paper, the *Neue Rheinische Zeitung*. There is good evidence that he was instrumental in dissolving the Communist League as incompatible with the more moderate policies advocated by his paper. Although the League was reconstituted in London in 1850, with Marx again as a leading member, it was dissolved again, at Marx's suggestion, two years later. Then followed two decades of conservative dominance in Europe, but with the growth of socialist parties during the last third of the century, the *Manifesto* emerged as a classic statement of the increasingly influential Marxist version of socialism. The Paris Commune prompted a hurried reprint of the German original in 1872, in the Preface to which Marx and Engels insisted that its general principles remained, on the whole, as correct as ever, although the ten-point programme would be very differently worded after twenty-five years, and, in particular, the simplistic attitude to the state as simply a neutral instrument of class-power would have to be radically emended. And the Russian edition of 1882 (the last published writing of Marx) proclaimed the possibility of a successful socialist revolution there—provided it were complemented by similar revolutions in Western Europe.

As Marx and Engels themselves later conceded, the *Manifesto* belongs to the springtime of socialist thought. As a propaganda document, some of its theses are undoubtedly simplistic. When they dealt with class-polarization, Marx and Engels must have been projecting the future tendencies that they saw at work in the present. In Germany at that time the proletariat in fact comprised less than 5 per cent of the population, and even in England the rule of the bourgeoisie was far from being 'universal'. Whether the working class in capitalist countries has been impoverished, even in relative terms, has been the subject of much controversy. And the prediction of a socialist revolution in Germany proved wide of the mark—though the same analysis was applied to Russia of the early 1900s, with greater accuracy, by Trotsky. But this is merely to say that, like all such documents, the *Manifesto* was a child of its time. In a sense, of course, virtually all the ideas contained in the *Manifesto* had been enunciated before—particularly among French socialists in whose tradition the *Manifesto* is firmly situated. Babeuf's ideas on revolution, Saint-Simon's periodization of history and emphasis on history, Considerant's *Manifeste*, all inspired aspects of the work of Marx and Engels. And Marx himself was the first to admit that the concept he began with—that of class—was used long before by French bourgeois historians. But the powerful, all-embracing synthesis and the consistently materialist approach were quite new. The *Manifesto* combines the genres of dramatic theatre with historical analysis. The result is a classic whose powerful vision has inspired generations of militants.

NOTE ON THE TEXT

The text used here is the translation made in 1888 by the translator of Marx's *Capital*, Samuel Moore, and supervised by Engels who added a few notes. Moore used the second German edition of 1872. The first German edition appeared in February 1848 in London, printed by Jacob Burghard of Bishopsgate, under the auspices of the German Workers Educational Association. A corrected version, eliminating the many printers' errors of the first, appeared in April of the same year. Both these versions were published anonymously. Moore's version, which has become the classic translation, frequently departs slightly from the original German and has been emended where necessary to be faithful to the original.

SELECT BIBLIOGRAPHY

Text

The present translation is largely that of Samuel Moore published in 1888 (see the 'Note on the Text'). Moore's unaltered text is reprinted in the editions by Struik, Taylor, Sweezy and Huberman, and the numerous Moscow editions. It is also reprinted in the Marx/Engels *Collected Works* (London, 1976), vol. 6, but with footnotes detailing the differences from the German original.

The first English translation was made by Helen Macfarlane and published in the Chartist newspaper *The Red Republican* in 1850. It is a somewhat fanciful version, as may be judged from its rendering of the opening sentence: 'A frightful hobgoblin stalks throughout Europe ...'. A somewhat more idiomatic and accurate translation than either Macfarlane or Moore is that of Eden and Cedar Paul, published in the Riazanov edition of 1930.

The most substantial bibliographical account of the early history of the *Manifesto* is contained in the massive volume by Bert Andreas, *Le Manifeste Communiste de Marx et Engels: Histoire et Bibliographie 1848–1918* (Milan, 1963).

Commentaries

ANDLER, CHARLES, *Le Manifeste Communiste: Introduction historique et commentaire* (Paris, 1901). Useful, although over-emphatic, on the French sources of the *Manifesto*.

CARR, E. H., *Studies in Revolution* (London, 1950), ch. 6. A good historical analysis.

CARVER, TERRELL, *Marx and Engels: The Intellectual Relationship* (Brighton, 1983), ch. 3. Emphasizes, by a detailed comparison of texts, Engels's contribution to the *Manifesto*.

GILBERT, ALAN, *Marx's Politics: Communists and Citizens* (Oxford, 1981). A vigorous and well-argued defence of the coherence of the strategy advocated in the *Manifesto*.

HUNLEY, J. D., *The Life and Thought of Friedrich Engels* (New Haven, 1991), ch. 4. Takes issue with Carver by claiming the essential similarity of the views of Marx and Engels.

HUNT, RICHARD, *The Political Ideas of Marx and Engels. Volume One: Marxism and Totalitarian Democracy 1818–1850* (London, 1974), chs. 5, 6, and 8. Good on the relationship between the history of the Communist League and the political strategy of Marx and Engels.

LASKI, HAROLD, *Harold Laski on the Communist Manifesto* (New York, 1967). Sets out to demonstrate congruity between the principles of the *Manifesto* and the policies of the British Labour Party.

RIAZANOV, DAVID, *The Communist Manifesto of Karl Marx and Friedrich Engels* (New York, 1930). A good historical introduction.

STRUIK, DIRK, *The Birth of the Communist Manifesto* (New York, 1971). In spite of the editor's annoyingly dogmatic Marxism, this is a most useful edition, with Engels's early drafts and good explanatory notes.

SWEEZY, PAUL and HUBERMAN, LEO, *The Communist Manifesto* (New York, 1964). Contains a measured historical commentary.

TAYLOR, A. J. P., *The Communist Manifesto* (Harmondsworth, 1967). Places the *Manifesto* excellently in the revolutionary context of the time. Written with great verve, but not with great accuracy.

WAGNER, Y. and STRAUSS, M., 'The Programme of the Communist Manifesto and its Political Implications', *Political Studies* (1969). An ingenious examination of the political and economic implications of the ten-point programme.

A CHRONOLOGY OF THE COMMUNIST MANIFESTO

1818 Marx born in Trier.

1820 Engels born in Barmen.

1836 Marx begins studying in Berlin.

1842 Marx becomes editor of *Rheinische Zeitung*; meets Engels briefly.

1843 Marx marries Jenny von Westphalen and moves to Paris and writes (1844) *Economic and Philosophical Manuscripts*. Engels works in his father's firm in Manchester.

1844 Marx and Engels meet in September and decide on full co-operation.

1845 Marx and Engels move to Brussels, and set up Communist Correspondence Committees. Engels publishes *The Condition of the Working Class in England*.

1846 Marx and Engels write *The German Ideology*.

1847 Engels attends Congress of Communist League in London in June. Marx and Engels both attend a second Congress there in December and are commissioned to write a manifesto.

1848 Marx finishes *Manifesto* in January and it is published in February. Revolution breaks out in Paris and Berlin. Marx and Engels move to Cologne where Marx becomes editor of *Neue Rheinische Zeitung*.

1849 On the collapse of the revolutionary movement, Marx settles in London to work on his critique of political economy.

1850 Engels moves to Manchester where he works for the next two decades.

1864 Marx helps to found the First International.

1867 Publication of Volume One of *Capital*.

1870 Engels retires from business and comes to live in London.

1871   The Paris Commune.

1872   Second German edition of the *Manifesto*.

1881   Death of Jenny Marx.

1882   Marx and Engels write Preface to the Second Russian edition of the *Manifesto*.

1883   Death of Marx. Burial in Highgate Cemetery.

1888   Preface to the English edition of the *Manifesto*.

1895   Death of Engels in London. Ashes scattered off Beachy Head, Eastbourne.

Manifesto of the Communist Party

MANIFESTO OF
THE COMMUNIST PARTY

A spectre is haunting Europe – the spectre of Communism. All the Powers of old Europe have entered into a holy alliance to exorcize this spectre: Pope and Czar, Metternich and Guizot, French Radicals and German police spies.

Where is the party in opposition that has not been decried as Communistic by its opponents in power? Where the Opposition that has not hurled back the branding reproach of Communism, against the more advanced opposition parties, as well as against its reactionary adversaries?

Two things result from this fact:

I. Communism is already acknowledged by all European Powers to be itself a Power.

II. It is high time that Communists should openly, in the face of the whole world, publish their views, their aims, their tendencies, and meet this nursery tale of the Spectre of Communism with a Manifesto of the party itself.

To this end, Communists of various nationalities have assembled in London, and sketched the following Manifesto, to be published in the English, French, German, Italian, Flemish and Danish languages.

I

Bourgeois and Proletarians*

THE history of all hitherto existing society* is the history of class struggles.

Freeman and slave, patrician and plebeian, lord and serf, guild-master* and journeyman, in a word, oppressor and oppressed, stood in constant opposition to one another, carried on an uninterrupted, now hidden, now open fight, a fight that each time ended, either in a revolutionary reconstitution of society at large, or in the common ruin of the contending classes.

In the earlier epochs of history, we find almost everywhere a complicated arrangement of society into various orders, a manifold gradation of social rank. In ancient Rome we have patricians, knights, plebeians, slaves; in the Middle Ages, feudal lords, vassals, guild-masters, journeymen, serfs; in almost all of these classes, again, subordinate gradations.

The modern bourgeois society that has sprouted from the ruins of feudal society has not done away with class antagonisms. It has but established new classes, new conditions of oppression, new forms of struggle in place of the old ones.

Our epoch, the epoch of the bourgeoisie, possesses, however, this distinctive feature: it has simplified the class antagonisms. Society as a whole is more and more splitting up into two great hostile camps, into two great classes directly facing each other: Bourgeoisie and Proletariat.

From the serfs of the Middle Ages sprang the chartered burghers of the earliest towns. From these burgesses the first elements of the bourgeoisie were developed.

The discovery of America, the rounding of the Cape, opened

up fresh ground for the rising bourgeoisie. The East-Indian and Chinese markets, the colonization of America, trade with the colonies, the increase in the means of exchange and in commodities generally, gave to commerce, to navigation, to industry, an impulse never before known, and thereby, to the revolutionary element in the tottering feudal society, a rapid development.

The previous feudal or guild organization of industry, under which industrial production was monopolized by closed guilds, now no longer sufficed for the growing wants of the new markets. The manufacturing system took its place. The guild-masters were pushed on one side by the manufacturing middle class; division of labour between the different corporate guilds vanished in the face of division of labour in each single workshop.

Meantime the markets kept ever growing, the demand ever rising. Even manufacture no longer sufficed. Thereupon, steam and machinery revolutionized industrial production. The place of manufacture was taken by the giant, Modern Industry, the place of the industrial middle class, by industrial millionaires, the leaders of whole industrial armies, the modern bourgeois.

Large-scale industry has established the world market, for which the discovery of America paved the way. This market has given an immense development to commerce, to navigation, to communication by land. This development has, in its turn, reacted on the extension of industry; and in proportion as industry, commerce, navigation, railways extended, in the same proportion the bourgeoisie developed, increased its capital, and pushed into the background every class handed down from the Middle Ages.

We see, therefore, how the modern bourgeoisie is itself the product of a long course of development, of a series of revolutions in the modes of production and of exchange.

Each step in the development of the bourgeoisie was accompanied by a corresponding political advance. An oppressed class under the sway of the feudal nobility, an armed and self-governing association in the medieval commune;* here independent urban republic, there taxable 'third estate' of the monarchy, afterwards, in the period of manufacture proper, serving either the estate or the absolute monarchy as a counterpoise against the nobility, and, in fact, corner-stone of the great monarchies in general, the bourgeoisie has at last, since the establishment of Modern Industry and of the world market, conquered for itself, in the modern representative State, exclusive political sway. The executive of the modern State is but a committee for managing the common affairs of the whole bourgeoisie.

The bourgeoisie, historically, has played a most revolutionary part.

The bourgeoisie, wherever it has got the upper hand, has put an end to all feudal, patriarchal, idyllic relations. It has pitilessly torn asunder the motley feudal ties that bound man to his 'natural superiors', and has left remaining no other nexus between man and man than naked self-interest, than callous 'cash payment'. It has drowned the most heavenly ecstasies of religious fervour, of chivalrous enthusiasm, of philistine sentimentalism, in the icy water of egotistical calculation. It has resolved personal worth into exchange value, and in place of the numberless indefeasible chartered freedoms, has set up that single, unconscionable freedom – Free Trade. In one word, for exploitation, veiled by religious and political illusions, it has substituted naked, shameless, direct, brutal exploitation.

The bourgeoisie has stripped of its halo every occupation hitherto honoured and looked up to with reverent awe. It has converted the physician, the lawyer, the priest, the poet, the man of science, into its paid wage-labourers.

The bourgeoisie has torn away from the family its sentimental veil, and has reduced the family relation to a mere money relation.

The bourgeoisie has disclosed how it came to pass that the brutal display of vigour in the Middle Ages, which Reactionists so much admire, found its fitting complement in the most slothful indolence. It has been the first to show what man's activity can bring about. It has accomplished wonders far surpassing Egyptian pyramids, Roman aqueducts, and Gothic cathedrals; it has conducted expeditions that put in the shade all former Exoduses of nations and crusades.

The bourgeoisie cannot exist without constantly revolutionizing the instruments of production, and thereby the relations of production, and with them the whole relations of society. Conservation of the old modes of production in unaltered form, was, on the contrary, the first condition of existence for all earlier industrial classes. Constant revolutionizing of production, uninterrupted disturbance of all social conditions, everlasting uncertainty and agitation distinguish the bourgeois epoch from all earlier ones. All fixed, fast-frozen relations, with their train of ancient and venerable prejudices and opinions are swept away, all new-formed ones become antiquated before they can ossify. All that is solid melts into air, all that is holy is profaned, and man is at last compelled to face with sober senses, his real conditions of life, and his relations with his kind.

The need of a constantly expanding market for its products chases the bourgeoisie over the whole surface of the globe. It must nestle everywhere, settle everywhere, establish connexions everywhere.

The bourgeoisie has through its exploitation of the world market given a cosmopolitan character to production and consumption in every country. To the great chagrin of Reactionists, it has drawn from under the feet of industry the national ground on which it stood. All old-established national industries have been destroyed or are daily being destroyed. They are dislodged by new industries, whose introduction becomes a life and death question for all civilized nations, by industries that no longer work up indigenous raw material, but raw material drawn from the remotest zones; industries whose products are consumed, not only at home, but in every quarter of the globe. In place of the old wants, satisfied by the productions of the country, we find new wants, requiring for their satisfaction the products of distant lands and climes. In place of the old local and national seclusion and self-sufficiency, we have intercourse in every direction, universal inter-dependence of nations. And as in material, so also in intellectual production. The intellectual creations of individual nations become common property. National one-sidedness and narrow-mindedness become more and more impossible, and from the numerous national and local literatures, there arises a world literature.

The bourgeoisie, by the rapid improvement of all instruments of production, by the immensely facilitated means of communication, draws all, even the most barbarian, nations into civilization. The cheap prices of its commodities are the heavy artillery with which it batters down all Chinese walls, with which it forces the barbarians' intensely obstinate hatred of foreigners to capitulate. It compels all nations, on pain of extinction, to adopt the bourgeois mode of production; it compels them to introduce what it calls civilization into their midst, i.e., to become bourgeois themselves. In one word, it creates a world after its own image.

The bourgeoisie has subjected the country to the rule of the towns. It has created enormous cities, has greatly increased the urban population as compared with the rural, and has thus rescued a considerable part of the population from the idiocy of rural life. Just as it has made the country dependent on the towns, so it has made barbarian and semi-barbarian countries dependent on the civilized ones, nations of peasants on nations of bourgeois, the East on the West.

The bourgeoisie keeps more and more doing away with the scattered state of the population, of the means of production, and of property. It has agglomerated population, centralized means of production, and has concentrated property in a few hands. The necessary consequence of this was political centralization. Independent, or but loosely connected, provinces with separate interests, laws, governments and systems of taxation, became lumped together into one nation, with one government, one code of laws, one national class-interest, one frontier and one customs-tariff.

The bourgeoisie, during its rule of scarce one hundred years, has created more massive and more colossal productive forces than have all preceding generations together. Subjection of Nature's forces to man, machinery, application of chemistry to industry and agriculture, steam-navigation, railways, electric telegraphs, clearing of whole continents for cultivation, canalization of rivers, whole populations conjured out of the ground – what earlier century had even a presentiment that such productive forces slumbered in the lap of social labour?

We see then: the means of production and of exchange, on whose foundation the bourgeoisie built itself up, were generated in feudal society. At a certain stage in the development of these means of production and of exchange, the conditions under which feudal society produced and exchanged, the feudal organization of agriculture and manufacturing industry, in one word, the feudal relations of property became no longer compatible with the already developed productive forces; they hindered production rather than advancing it; they became so many fetters. They had to be burst asunder; they were burst asunder.

Into their place stepped free competition, accompanied by a social and political constitution adapted to it, and by the economical and political sway of the bourgeois class.

A similar movement is going on before our own eyes. Modern bourgeois society with its relations of production, of exchange and of property, a society that has conjured up such gigantic means of production and of exchange, is like the sorcerer, who is no longer able to control the powers of the nether world whom he has called up by his spells. For many a decade past the history of industry and commerce is but the history of the revolt of modern productive forces against modern conditions of production, against the property relations that are the conditions for the existence of the bourgeoisie and of its rule. It is enough to mention the commercial crises that by their periodical return put on its trial, each time more threateningly, the existence of the entire bourgeois society. In these crises a great part not only of the existing products, but also of the previously created productive forces, are periodically destroyed. In these crises there breaks out a social epidemic that, in all earlier epochs, would have seemed an absurdity – the epidemic of over-production. Society suddenly finds itself put back into a state of momentary barbarism; it appears as if a famine, a universal war of devastation had cut off the supply of every means of subsistence; industry and commerce seem to be destroyed; and why? Because there is too much civilization, too much means of subsistence, too much industry, too much commerce. The productive forces at the disposal of society no longer tend to further the development of bourgeois civilization and the conditions of bourgeois property; on the contrary, they have become too powerful for these conditions, by which they are fettered, and so soon as they overcome these fetters, they bring disorder into the whole of bourgeois society, endanger the existence of bourgeois property. The conditions of bourgeois society are too narrow to comprise the wealth created by them. And how does the bourgeoisie get over these crises? On the one hand by enforced destruction of a mass of productive forces; on the other, by the conquest of new markets, and by the more thorough exploitation of the old ones. That is to say, by paving the way for more extensive and more destructive crises, and by diminishing the means whereby crises are prevented.

The weapons with which the bourgeoisie felled feudalism to the ground are now turned against the bourgeoisie itself.

But not only has the bourgeoisie forged the weapons that bring death to itself; it has also called into existence the men who are to wield those weapons – the modern workers – the proletarians.

In proportion as the bourgeoisie, i.e., capital, is developed, in the same proportion is the proletariat, the modern working class, developed – a class of labourers, who live only so long as they find work, and who find work only so long as their labour increases capital. These labourers, who must sell themselves piecemeal, are a commodity, like every other article of commerce, and are consequently exposed to all the vicissitudes of competition, to all the fluctuations of the market.

Owing to the extensive use of machinery and to division of

labour, the work of the proletarians has lost all individual character, and, consequently, all charm for the workman. He becomes an appendage of the machine, and it is only the most simple, most monotonous, and most easily acquired knack, that is required of him. Hence, the cost of production of a workman is restricted, almost entirely, to the means of subsistence that he requires for his maintenance, and for the propagation of his race. But the price of a commodity, and therefore also of labour, is equal to its cost of production. In proportion, therefore, as the repulsiveness of the work increases, the wage decreases. Nay more, in proportion as the use of machinery and division of labour increases, in the same proportion the quantity of labour also increases, whether by prolongation of the working hours, by increase of the work exacted in a given time or by increased speed of the machinery, etc.

Modern industry has converted the little workshop of the patriarchal master into the great factory of the industrial capitalist. Masses of labourers, crowded into the factory, are organized like soldiers. As privates of the industrial army they are placed under the command of a perfect hierarchy of officers and sergeants. Not only are they slaves of the bourgeois class, and of the bourgeois State; they are daily and hourly enslaved by the machine, by the overlooker, and, above all, by the individual bourgeois manufacturer himself. The more openly this despotism proclaims gain to be its end and aim, the more petty, the more hateful and the more embittering it is.

The less the skill and exertion of strength implied in manual labour, in other words, the more modern industry becomes developed, the more is the labour of men superseded by that of women. Differences of age and sex have no longer any distinctive social validity for the working class. All are instruments of labour, more or less expensive to use, according to their age and sex.

No sooner is the exploitation of the labourer by the manufacturer, so far, at an end, that he receives his wages in cash, than he is set upon by the other portions of the bourgeoisie, the landlord, the shopkeeper, the pawnbroker, etc.

The former lower strata of the middle estate – the small tradespeople, shopkeepers, and rentiers, the handicraftsmen and peasants – all these sink gradually into the proletariat, partly because their diminutive capital does not suffice for the scale on which Modern Industry is carried on, and is swamped in the competition with the large capitalists, partly because their specialized skill is rendered worthless by new methods of production. Thus the proletariat is recruited from all classes of the population.

The proletariat goes through various stages of development. With its birth begins its struggle with the bourgeoisie. At first the contest is carried on by individual labourers, then by the workpeople of a factory, then by the operatives of one trade, in one locality, against the individual bourgeois who directly exploits them. They direct their attacks not only against the bourgeois conditions of production, they direct them against the instruments of production themselves; they destroy imported wares that compete with their labour, they smash to pieces machinery, they set factories ablaze, they seek to restore by force the vanished status of the workman of the Middle Ages.

At this stage the labourers still form a mass scattered over the whole country, and broken up by their mutual competition. If anywhere they unite to form more compact bodies, this is not yet the consequence of their own active union, but of the union of the bourgeoisie, which class, in order to attain its own political ends, is compelled to set the whole proletariat in motion, and is moreover yet, for a time, able to do so. At this stage, therefore, the proletarians do not fight their enemies, but the enemies of their enemies, the remnants of absolute monarchy, the landowners, the non-industrial bourgeois, the petty bourgeoisie. Thus the whole historical movement is concentrated in the hands of the bourgeoisie; every victory so obtained is a victory for the bourgeoisie.

But with the development of industry the proletariat not only increases in number; it becomes concentrated in greater masses, its strength grows, and it feels that strength more. The various interests and conditions of life within the ranks of the proletariat are more and more equalized, in proportion as machinery obliterates all distinctions of labour, and nearly everywhere reduces wages to the same low level. The growing competition among the bourgeois, and the resulting commercial crises, make the wages of the workers ever more fluctuating. The unceasing improvement of machinery, ever more rapidly developing, makes their livelihood more and more precarious; the collisions between individual workmen and individual bourgeois take more and more the character of collisions between two classes. Thereupon the workers begin to form combinations against the bourgeois; they club together in order to keep up the rate of wages; they found permanent associations in order to make provision beforehand for these occasional revolts. Here and there the contest breaks out into riots.

Now and then the workers are victorious, but only for a time. The real fruit of their battles lies, not in the immediate result, but in the ever-expanding union of the workers. This union is helped on by the improved means of communication that are created by modern industry and that place the workers of different localities in contact with one another. It was just this contact that was needed to centralize the numerous local struggles, all of the same character, into one national struggle between classes. But every class struggle is a political struggle. And that union, to attain which the burghers of the Middle Ages, with their miserable highways, required centuries, the modern proletarians, thanks to railways, achieve in a few years.

This organization of the proletarians into a class, and consequently into a political party, is continually being upset again by the competition between the workers themselves. But it ever rises up again, stronger, firmer, mightier. It compels legislative recognition of particular interests of the workers, by taking advantage of the divisions among the bourgeoisie itself. Thus the Ten Hours bill in England was carried.*

Although collisions between the classes of the old society further, in many ways, the course of development of the proletariat.

The bourgeoisie finds itself involved in a constant battle. At first with the aristocracy; later on, with those portions of the bourgeoisie itself, whose interests have become antagonistic to the progress of industry; at all times, with the bourgeoisie of foreign countries. In all these battles it sees itself compelled to appeal to the proletariat, to ask for its help, and thus, to drag it into the political arena. The bourgeoisie itself, therefore, supplies the proletariat with its own elements of education, in other words, it furnishes the proletariat with weapons for fighting the bourgeoisie.

Further, as we have already seen, entire sections of the ruling classes are, by the advance of industry, precipitated into the proletariat, or are at least threatened in their conditions of existence. These also supply the proletariat with a lot of elements of education.

Finally, in times when the class struggle nears the decisive hour, the process of dissolution going on within the ruling class, in fact within the whole range of old society, assumes such a violent, glaring character, that a small section of the ruling class cuts itself adrift, and joins the revolutionary class, the class that holds the future in its hands. Just as, therefore, at an earlier period, a section of the nobility went over to the bourgeoisie, so now a portion of the bourgeoisie goes over to the proletariat, and in particular, a portion of the bourgeois ideologists, who have raised themselves to the level of comprehending theoretically the historical movement as a whole.

Of all the classes that stand face to face with the bourgeoisie today, the proletariat alone is a really revolutionary class. The other classes decay and finally disappear in the face of modern industry; the proletariat is its special and essential product.

The middle estates, the small manufacturer, the shopkeeper, the artisan, the peasant, all these fight against the bourgeoisie, to save from extinction their existence as fractions of the middle class. They are therefore not revolutionary, but conservative. Nay more, they are reactionary, for they try to roll back the wheel of history. If by chance they are revolutionary, they are so only in view of their impending transfer into the proletariat, they thus defend not their present, but their future interests, they desert their own standpoint to place themselves at that of the proletariat.

The lumpenproletariat, that passively rotting mass thrown off by the lowest layers of old society, may, here and there, be swept into the movement by a proletarian revolution; its conditions of life, however, prepare it far more for the part of a bribed tool of reactionary intrigue.

In the conditions of the proletariat, those of old society at large are already virtually swamped. The proletarian is without property; his relation to his wife and children has no longer anything in common with the bourgeois family relations; modern industrial labour, modern subjection to capital, the same in England as in France, in America as in Germany, has stripped him of every trace of national character. Law, morality, religion, are to him so many bourgeois prejudices, behind which lurk in ambush just as many bourgeois interests.

All the preceding classes that got the upper hand sought to fortify their already acquired status by subjecting society at large to their conditions of appropriation. The proletarians cannot become masters of the productive forces of society, except by abolishing their own previous mode of appropriation, and thereby also every other previous mode of appropriation. They have nothing of their own to secure and to fortify; their mission is to destroy all previous securities for, and insurances of, individual property.

All previous historical movements were movements of minorities, or in the interest of minorities. The proletarian movement is the independent movement of the immense majority, in the interest of the immense majority. The proletariat, the lowest stratum of our present society, cannot stir, cannot raise itself up, without the whole superincumbent strata of official society being sprung into the air.

Though not in substance, yet in form, the struggle of the proletariat with the bourgeoisie is at first a national struggle. The proletariat of each country must, of course, first of all settle matters with its own bourgeoisie.

In depicting the most general phases of the development of the proletariat, we traced the more or less veiled civil war, raging within existing society, up to the point where that war breaks out into open revolution, and where the violent overthrow of the bourgeoisie lays the foundation for the sway of the proletariat.

Hitherto, every form of society has been based, as we have already seen, on the antagonism of oppressing and oppressed classes. But in order to oppress a class, certain conditions must be assured to it under which it can, at least, continue its slavish existence. The serf, in the period of serfdom, raised himself to membership in the commune, just as the petty bourgeois, under the yoke of feudal absolutism, managed to develop into a bourgeois. The modern labourer, on the contrary, instead of rising with the progress of industry, sinks deeper and deeper below the conditions of existence of his own class. He becomes a pauper, and pauperism develops more rapidly than population and wealth. And here it becomes evident, that the bourgeoisie is unfit any longer to be the ruling class in society, and to impose its conditions of existence upon society as an overriding law. It is unfit to rule because it is incompetent to assure an existence to its slave within his slavery, because it cannot help letting him sink into such a state, that it has to feed him, instead of being fed by him. Society can no longer live under this bourgeoisie, in other words, its existence is no longer compatible with society.

The essential condition for the existence, and for the sway of the bourgeois class, is the accumulation of wealth in the hands of private individuals, the formation and augmentation of capital; the condition for capital is wage labour. Wage labour rests exclusively on competition between the labourers. The advance of industry, whose involuntary promoter is the bourgeoisie, replaces the isolation of the labourers, due to competition, by their revolutionary combination, due to association. The development of Modern Industry, therefore, cuts from under its feet the very foundation on which the bourgeoisie produces and appropriates products. What the bourgeoisie, therefore, produces, above all, is its own grave-diggers. Its fall and the victory of the proletariat are equally inevitable.

2

Proletarians and Communists

IN what relation do the Communists stand to the proletarians as a whole?

The Communists do not form a separate party opposed to other working-class parties.

They have no interest separate and apart from those of the proletariat as a whole.

They do not set up any separate principles of their own, by which to shape and mould the proletarian movement.

The Communists are distinguished from the other working-class parties by this only: 1. In the national struggles of the proletarians of the different countries, they point out and bring to the front the common interests of the entire proletariat, independently of all nationality. 2. In the various stages of development which the struggle of the working class against the bourgeoisie has to pass through, they always and everywhere represent the interests of the movement as a whole.

The Communists, therefore, are on the one hand, practically, the most resolute section of the working-class parties of every country, that section which pushes forward all others; on the other hand, theoretically, they have over the great mass of the proletariat the advantage of clearly understanding the line of march, the conditions, and the ultimate general results of the proletarian movement.

The immediate aim of the Communists is the same as that of all the other proletarian parties: formation of the proletariat into a class, overthrow of the bourgeois supremacy, conquest of political power by the proletariat.

The theoretical conclusions of the Communists are in no way based on ideas or principles that have been invented, or discovered, by this or that would-be universal reformer.

They merely express, in general terms, actual relations springing from an existing class struggle, from a historical movement going on under our very eyes. The abolition of existing property relations is not at all a distinctive feature of Communism.

All property relations in the past were subject to constant historical replacement, constant historical change.

The French Revolution, for example, abolished feudal property in favour of bourgeois property.

The distinguishing feature of Communism is not the abolition of property generally, but the abolition of bourgeois property. But modern bourgeois private property is the final and most complete expression of the system of producing and appropriating products, that is based on class antagonisms, on the exploitation of some by others.

In this sense, the theory of the Communists may be summed up in the single sentence: Abolition of private property.

We Communists have been reproached with the desire of abolishing the right of personally acquiring property as the fruit of a man's own labour, which property is alleged to be the ground work of all personal freedom, activity and independence.

Hard-won, self-acquired, self-earned property! Do you mean the property of the petty bourgeois and of the small peasant, a form of property that preceded the bourgeois form? There is no need to abolish that; the development of industry has to a great extent already destroyed it, and is still destroying it daily.

Or do you mean modern bourgeois private property?

But does wage labour create any property for the labourer? Not a bit. It creates capital, i.e., that kind of property which exploits wage labour, and which cannot increase except upon condition of begetting a new supply of wage labour for fresh exploitation. Property, in its present form, is based on the antagonism of capital and wage labour. Let us examine both sides of this antagonism.

To be a capitalist is to have not only a purely personal but a social *status* in production. Capital is a collective product, and only by the united action of many members, nay, in the last resort, only by the united action of all members of society, can it be set in motion.

Capital is, therefore, not a personal, it is a social power.

When, therefore, capital is converted into common property, into the property of all members of society, personal property is not thereby transformed into social property. It is only the social character of the property that is changed. It loses its class character.

Let us now take wage labour.

The average price of wage labour is the minimum wage, i.e., that quantum of the means of subsistence which is absolutely requisite to keep the labourer in bare existence as a labourer. What, therefore, the wage-labourer appropriates by means of his labour, merely suffices to prolong and reproduce a bare existence. We by no means intend to abolish this personal appropriation of the products of labour, an appropriation that is made for the maintenance and reproduction of human life, and that leaves no surplus wherewith to command the labour of others. All that we want to do away with is the miserable character of this appropriation, under which the labourer lives merely to increase capital, and is allowed to live only in so far as the interest of the ruling class requires it.

In bourgeois society, living labour is but a means to increase accumulated labour. In Communist society, accumulated labour is but a means to widen, to enrich, to promote the existence of the labourer.

In bourgeois society, therefore, the past dominates the present; in Communist society, the present dominates the past. In bourgeois society capital is independent and has individuality, while the living person is dependent and has no individuality.

And the abolition of this state of things is called by the bourgeois, abolition of individuality and freedom! And rightly so. The abolition of bourgeois individuality, bourgeois independence, and bourgeois freedom is undoubtedly aimed at.

By freedom is meant, under the present bourgeois conditions of production, free trade, free selling and buying.

But if selling and buying disappears, free selling and buying disappears also. This talk about free selling and buying, and all the other 'brave words' of our bourgeoisie about freedom in general, have a meaning, if any, only in contrast with restricted selling and buying, with the fettered traders of the Middle Ages, but have no meaning when opposed to the Communistic abolition of buying and selling, of the bourgeois conditions of production, and of the bourgeoisie itself.

You are horrified at our intending to do away with private property. But in your existing society, private property is already done away with for nine-tenths of the population; its existence is solely due to its non-existence in the hands of those nine-tenths. You reproach us, therefore, with intending to do away with a form of property the necessary condition for whose existence is the non-existence of any property for the immense majority of society.

In one word, you reproach us with intending to do away with your property. Precisely so; that is just what we intend.

From the moment when labour can no longer be converted into capital, money, or rent, into a social power capable of being monopolized, i.e., from the moment when individual property can no longer be transformed into bourgeois property, from that moment, you say, individuality vanishes.

You must, therefore, confess that by 'individual' you mean no other person than the bourgeois, than the middle-class owner of property. This person must, indeed, be swept out of the way.

Communism deprives no man of the power to appropriate the products of society; all that it does is to deprive him of the power to subjugate the labour of others by means of such appropriation.

It has been objected that upon the abolition of private property all work will cease, and universal laziness will overtake us.

According to this, bourgeois society ought long ago to have gone to the dogs through sheer idleness; for those of its members who work, acquire nothing, and those who acquire anything, do not work. The whole of this objection is but another expression of the tautology: that there can no longer be any wage labour when there is no longer any capital.

All objections urged against the Communistic mode of producing and appropriating material products, have, in the same way, been urged against the Communistic modes of producing and appropriating intellectual products. Just as, to the bourgeois, the disappearance of class property is the disappearance of production itself, so the disappearance of class culture is to him identical with the disappearance of all culture.

That culture, the loss of which he laments, is, for the enormous majority, a mere training to act as a machine.

But don't wrangle with us so long as you apply, to the abolition of bourgeois property, the standard of your bourgeois notions of freedom, culture, law, &c. Your very ideas are but the outgrowth of the conditions of your bourgeois production and bourgeois property, just as your jurisprudence is but the will of your class made into a law for all, a will, whose essential content is determined by the material conditions of existence of your class.

The selfish conception that induces you to transform into eternal laws of nature and of reason, the social forms springing from your present mode of production and form of property – historical relations that rise and disappear in the progress of production – this conception you share with every ruling class that has disappeared. What you see clearly in the case of ancient property, what you admit in the case of feudal property, you are of course forbidden to admit in the case of your own bourgeois form of property.

Abolition of the family! Even the most radical flare up at this infamous proposal of the Communists.

On what foundation is the present family, the bourgeois

family, based? On capital, on private gain. In its completely developed form this family exists only among the bourgeoisie. But this state of things finds its complement in the practical absence of the family among the proletarians, and in public prostitution.

The bourgeois family will vanish as a matter of course when its complement vanishes, and both will vanish with the vanishing of capital.

Do you charge us with wanting to stop the exploitation of children by their parents? To this crime we plead guilty.

But, you will say, we destroy the most hallowed of relations, when we replace home education by social.

And your education! Is not that also social, and determined by the social conditions under which you educate, by the intervention, direct or indirect, of society, by means of schools, &c? The Communists have not invented the intervention of society in education; they do but seek to alter the character of that intervention, and to rescue education from the influence of the ruling class.

The bourgeois clap-trap about the family and education, about the hallowed co-relation of parent and child, becomes all the more disgusting, the more, by the action of Modern Industry, all family ties among the proletarians are torn asunder, and their children transformed into simple articles of commerce and instruments of labour.

But you Communists would introduce community of women, screams the whole bourgeoisie in chorus.

The bourgeois sees in his wife a mere instrument of production. He hears that the instruments of production are to be exploited in common, and, naturally, can come to no other conclusion than that the lot of being common to all will likewise fall to the women.

He has not even a suspicion that the real point aimed at is to do away with the status of women as mere instruments of production.

For the rest, nothing is more ridiculous than the virtuous

indignation of our bourgeois at the community of women which, they pretend, is to be openly and officially established by the Communists. The Communists have no need to introduce community of women; it has existed almost from time immemorial.

Our bourgeois, not content with having the wives and daughters of their proletarians at their disposal, not to speak of common prostitutes, take the greatest pleasure in seducing each other's wives.

Bourgeois marriage is in reality a system of wives in common and thus, at the most, what the Communists might possibly be reproached with, is that they desire to introduce, in substitution for a hypocritically concealed, an openly legalized community of women. For the rest, it is self-evident that the abolition of the present system of production must bring with it the abolition of the community of women springing from that system, i.e., of prostitution both public and private.

The Communists are further reproached with desiring to abolish countries and nationality.

The working men have no country. We cannot take from them what they have not got. Since the proletariat must first of all acquire political supremacy, must rise to be the national class, must constitute itself *the* nation, it is, so far, itself national, though not in the bourgeois sense of the word.

National differences and antagonisms between peoples are daily more and more vanishing, owing to the development of the bourgeoisie, to freedom of commerce, to the world market, to uniformity in the mode of production and in the conditions of life corresponding thereto.

The supremacy of the proletariat will cause them to vanish still faster. United action, of the leading civilized countries at least, is one of the first conditions for the emancipation of the proletariat.

In proportion as the exploitation of one individual by another is put an end to, the exploitation of one nation by another will also be put an end to. In proportion as the antagonism between classes within the nation vanishes, the hostility of one nation to another will come to an end.

The charges against Communism made from a religious, a philosophical, and, generally, from an ideological standpoint, are not deserving of serious examination.

Does it require deep intuition to comprehend that man's ideas, views and conceptions, in one word, man's consciousness, changes with every change in the conditions of his existence, in his social relations and in his social life?

What else does the history of ideas prove, than that intellectual production changes in character in proportion as material production is changed? The ruling ideas of each age have ever been the ideas of its ruling class.

When people speak of ideas that revolutionize society, they do but express the fact, that within the old society, the elements of a new one have been created, and that the dissolution of the old ideas keeps even pace with the dissolution of the old conditions of existence.

When the ancient world was in its last throes, the ancient religions were overcome by Christianity. When Christian ideas succumbed in the 18th century to the ideas of the Enlightenment, feudal society fought its death battle with the then revolutionary bourgeoisie. The ideas of religious liberty and freedom of conscience, merely gave expression to the sway of free competition within the domain of knowledge.

'Undoubtedly,' it will be said, 'religious, moral, philosophical, political, juridical ideas, etc., have been modified in the course of historical development. But religion, morality, philosophy, political science, and law, constantly survived this change.

'There are, besides, eternal truths, such as Freedom, Justice, etc., that are common to all states of society. But Communism abolishes eternal truths, it abolishes all religion, and all morality, instead of constituting them on a new basis; it therefore acts in contradiction to all past historical experience.'

What does this accusation reduce itself to? The history of all past society has consisted in the development of class antagonisms, antagonisms that assumed different forms at different epochs.

But whatever form they may have taken, one fact is common to all past ages, viz., the exploitation of one part of society by the other. No wonder, then, that the social consciousness of past ages, despite all the multiplicity and variety it displays, moves within certain common forms, in forms of consciousness which cannot completely vanish except with the total disappearance of class antagonisms.

The Communist revolution is the most radical rupture with traditional property relations; no wonder that its development involves the most radical rupture with traditional ideas.

But let us have done with the bourgeois objections to Communism.

We have seen above, that the first step in the revolution by the working class, is to raise the proletariat to the position of ruling class, to win the battle of democracy.

The proletariat will use its political supremacy to wrest, by degrees, all capital from the bourgeoisie, to centralize all instruments of production in the hands of the State, i.e., of the proletariat organized as the ruling class; and to increase the total of productive forces as rapidly as possible.

Of course, in the beginning, this cannot be effected except by means of despotic inroads on the rights of property, and on the conditions of bourgeois production; by means of measures, therefore, which appear economically insufficient and untenable, but which, in the course of the movement, outstrip themselves and are unavoidable as a means of entirely revolutionizing the mode of production.

These measures will of course be different in different countries.

Nevertheless, in the most advanced countries, the following will be pretty generally applicable:

1. Expropriation of property in land and application of all rents of land to public purposes.

2. A heavy progressive tax.

3. Abolition of all right of inheritance.

4. Confiscation of the property of all emigrants and rebels.

5. Centralization of credit in the hands of the State, by means of a national bank with State capital and an exclusive monopoly.

6. Centralization of transport in the hands of the State.

7. Extension of factories and instruments of production owned by the State; the bringing into cultivation of wastelands, and the improvement of the soil generally in accordance with a common plan.

8. Equal liability of all to labour. Establishment of industrial armies, especially for agriculture.

9. Combination of agriculture with industry, promotion of the gradual elimination of the contradictions between town and countryside.

10. Free education for all children in public schools. Abolition of children's factory labour in its present form. Combination of education with industrial production, &c., &c.

When, in the course of development, class distinctions have disappeared, and all production has been concentrated in the hands of associated individuals, the public power will lose its political character. Political power, properly so called, is merely the organized power of one class for oppressing another. If the proletariat during its contest with the bourgeoisie is compelled, by the force of circumstances, to organize itself as a class, if, by means of a revolution, it makes itself the ruling class, and, as such, sweeps away by force the old conditions of production, then it will, along with these conditions, have swept away the conditions for the existence of class antagonisms and of classes generally, and will thereby have abolished its own supremacy as a class.

In place of the old bourgeois society, with its classes and class antagonisms, we shall have an association, in which the free development of each is the condition for the free development of all.

3

Socialist and Communist Literature

I. REACTIONARY SOCIALISM

a. Feudal Socialism

OWING to their historical position, it became the vocation of the aristocracies of France and England to write pamphlets against modern bourgeois society. In the French revolution of July 1830, and in the English reform agitation,* these aristocracies again succumbed to the hateful upstart. Thenceforth, a serious political contest was altogether out of question. A literary battle alone remained possible. But even in the domain of literature the old cries of the restoration period* had become impossible.

In order to arouse sympathy, the aristocracy were obliged to lose sight, apparently, of their own interests, and to formulate their indictment against the bourgeoisie in the interest of the exploited working class alone. Thus the aristocracy took their revenge by singing lampoons on their new master, and whispering in his ears more or less sinister prophecies.

In this way arose feudal Socialism: half lamentation, half lampoon; half echo of the past, half menace of the future; at times, by its bitter, witty and incisive criticism, striking the bourgeoisie to the very heart's core; but always ludicrous in its effect, through total incapacity to comprehend the march of modern history.

The aristocracy, in order to rally the people to them, waved the proletarian alms-bag in front for a banner. But the people, so often as it joined them, saw on their hindquarters the old feudal coats of arms, and deserted with loud and irreverent laughter.

One section of the French Legitimists and 'Young England'* exhibited this spectacle.

In pointing out that their mode of exploitation was different to that of the bourgeoisie, the feudalists forget that they exploited under circumstances and conditions that were quite different, and that are now antiquated. In showing that, under their rule, the modern proletariat never existed, they forget that the modern bourgeoisie is the necessary offspring of their own form of society.

For the rest, so little do they conceal the reactionary character of their criticism that their chief accusation against the bourgeoisie amounts to this, that under the bourgeois *régime* a class is being developed, which is destined to cut up root and branch the old order of society.

What they upbraid the bourgeoisie with is not so much that it creates a proletariat, as that it creates a *revolutionary* proletariat.

In political practice, therefore, they join in all coercive measures against the working class; and in ordinary life, despite their high-falutin phrases, they stoop to pick up the golden apples, and to barter truth, love, and honour for traffic in wool, beetroot-sugar, and potato spirits.*

As the parson has ever gone hand in hand with the feudal lord, so has Clerical Socialism with Feudal Socialism.

Nothing is easier than to give Christian asceticism a Socialist tinge. Has not Christianity declaimed against private property, against marriage, against the State? Has it not preached in the place of these, charity and poverty, celibacy and mortification of the flesh, monastic life and Mother Church? Christian Socialism is but the holy water with which the priest consecrates the heart-burnings of the aristocrat.

b. Petty-Bourgeois Socialism

The feudal aristocracy was not the only class that was ruined by the bourgeoisie, not the only class whose conditions of existence pined and perished in the atmosphere of modern bourgeois society. The medieval burgesses and the small peasant proprietors were the precursors of the modern bourgeoisie. In those countries which are but little developed, industrially and commercially, this class still vegetates side by side with the rising bourgeoisie.

In countries where modern civilization has become fully developed, a new class of petty bourgeois has been formed, fluctuating between proletariat and bourgeoisie and ever renewing itself as a supplementary part of bourgeois society. The individual members of this class, however, are being constantly hurled down into the proletariat by the action of competition, and, as modern industry develops, they even see the moment approaching when they will completely disappear as an independent section of modern society, to be replaced, in manufacture, agriculture and commerce, by overlookers, bailiffs and shopmen.

In countries like France, where the peasants constitute far more than half of the population, it was natural that writers who sided with the proletariat against the bourgeoisie, should use, in their criticism of the bourgeois *régime*, the standard of the peasant and petty bourgeois, and from the standpoint of the petty bourgeoisie should take up the cudgels for the working class. Thus arose petty-bourgeois Socialism. Sismondi was the head of this school, not only in France but also in England.

This school of Socialism dissected with great acuteness the contradictions in the conditions of modern production. It laid bare the hypocritical apologies of economists. It proved, incontrovertibly, the disastrous effects of machinery and division of labour; the concentration of capital and land in a few hands; over-production and crises; it pointed out the inevitable ruin of the petty bourgeois and peasant, the misery of the proletariat, the anarchy in production, the crying inequalities in the distribution of wealth, the industrial war of extermination between nations, the dissolution of old moral bonds, of the old family relations, of the old nationalities.

In its positive aims, however, this form of Socialism aspires either to restoring the old means of production and of exchange, and with them the old property relations, and the old society, or to cramping the modern means of production and of exchange, within the framework of the old property relations that have been, and were bound to be, exploded by those means. In either case, it is both reactionary and Utopian.

Its last words are: corporate guilds for manufacture; patriarchal relations in agriculture.

In its further development, this trend ended in a cowardly fit of the blues.

c. German, or 'True', Socialism

The Socialist and Communist literature of France, a literature that originated under the pressure of a bourgeoisie in power, and that was the expression of the struggle against this power, was introduced into Germany at a time when the bourgeoisie, in that country, had just begun its contest with feudal absolutism.

German philosophers, semi-philosophers, and fine spirits, eagerly seized on this literature, only forgetting, that when these writings immigrated from France into Germany, French social conditions had not immigrated along with them. In contact with German social conditions, this French literature lost all its immediate practical significance, and assumed a purely literary aspect. It must have appeared as idle speculation on true society, on the realization of the human essence. Thus, to the German philosophers of the Eighteenth Century, the demands of the first French Revolution were nothing more than the demands of 'Practical Reason'* in general, and the utterance of the will of the revolutionary French bourgeoisie signified in their eyes the laws of pure Will, of Will as it was bound to be, of true human Will generally.

The work of the German *literati* consisted solely in bringing the new French ideas into harmony with their ancient philosophical conscience, or rather, in annexing the French ideas without deserting their own philosophic point of view.

This annexation took place in the same way in which a foreign language is appropriated, namely, by translation.

It is well known how the monks wrote silly lives of Catholic Saints *over* the manuscripts on which the classical works of ancient heathendom had been written. The German *literati* reversed this process with the profane French literature. They wrote their philosophical nonsense beneath the French original. For instance, beneath the French criticism of money relations, they wrote 'Alienation of Humanity', and beneath the French criticism of the bourgeois State they wrote, 'Transcendence of the domination of the abstractly General', etc.

The introduction of these philosophical phrases at the back of the French theories they dubbed 'Philosophy of Action', 'True Socialism', 'German Science of Socialism', 'Philosophical Foundation of Socialism', and so on.

The French Socialist and Communist literature was thus completely emasculated. And, since it ceased in the hands of the German to express the struggle of one class with the other, he felt conscious of having overcome 'French one-sidedness' and of representing, not true requirements, but the requirements of Truth; not the interests of the proletariat, but the interests of Human Nature, of Man in general, who belongs to no class, has no reality, who exists only in the misty realm of philosophical fantasy.

This German Socialism, which took its schoolboy task so seriously and solemnly, and extolled its poor stock-in-trade in such mountebank fashion, meanwhile gradually lost its pedantic innocence.

The fight of the German, and, especially of the Prussian bourgeoisie, against feudal aristocracy and absolute monarchy, in other words, the liberal movement, became more earnest.

By this, the long wished-for opportunity was offered to 'True' Socialism of confronting the political movement with the Socialist demands, of hurling the traditional anathemas against liberalism, against representative government, against bourgeois competition, bourgeois freedom of the press, bourgeois legislation, bourgeois liberty and equality, and of preaching to the masses that they had nothing to gain, and everything to lose, by

this bourgeois movement. German Socialism forgot, in the nick
of time, that the French criticism, whose silly echo it was, pre-
supposed the existence of modern bourgeois society, with its
corresponding material conditions of existence, and the political
constitution adapted thereto, the very things whose attainment
was the object of the pending struggle in Germany.

To the German absolute governments, with their following
of parsons, professors, country squires and officials, it served as a
welcome scarecrow against the threatening bourgeoisie.

It was a sweet finish after the bitter pills of floggings and bullets
with which these same governments dosed the German
working-class risings.

While this 'True' Socialism thus served the governments as a
weapon for fighting the German bourgeoisie, it, at the same
time, directly represented a reactionary interest, the interest of
the German Philistines. In Germany the *petty-bourgeois* class, a
relic of the sixteenth century, and since then constantly cropping
up again under various forms, is the real social basis of the existing state of things.

To preserve this class is to preserve the existing state of things
in Germany. The industrial and political supremacy of the bourgeoisie threatens it with certain destruction; on the one hand,
from the concentration of capital; on the other, from the rise of a
revolutionary proletariat. 'True' Socialism appeared to kill these
two birds with one stone. It spread like an epidemic.

The robe of speculative cobwebs, embroidered with flowers
of rhetoric, steeped in the dew of sickly sentiment, this transcen-
dental robe in which the German Socialists wrapped their sorry
'eternal truths', all skin and bone, served to wonderfully increase
the sale of their goods amongst such a public.

And on its part, German Socialism recognized, more and
more, its own calling as the bombastic representative of the
petty-bourgeois Philistine.

It proclaimed the German nation to be the model nation, and
the German petty Philistine to be the typical man. To every
villainous meanness of this model man it gave a hidden, higher,

Socialistic interpretation, the exact contrary of its real character. It went to the extreme length of directly opposing the 'brutally destructive' tendency of Communism, and of proclaiming its supreme and impartial contempt of all class struggles. With very few exceptions, all the so-called Socialist and Communist publications that now (1847) circulate in Germany belong to the domain of this foul and enervating literature.*

II. CONSERVATIVE, OR BOURGEOIS, SOCIALISM

A part of the bourgeoisie is desirous of redressing social griev-ances, in order to secure the continued existence of bourgeois society.

To this section belongs economists, philanthropists, humani-tarians, improvers of the condition of the working class, organ-isers of charity, members of societies for the prevention of cruelty to animals, temperance fanatics, hole-and-corner refor-mers of every imaginable kind. This form of Socialism has, moreover, been worked out into complete systems.

We may cite Proudhon's *Philosophie de la Misère* as an example of this form.*

The Socialistic bourgeois want the living conditions of modern society without the struggles and dangers necessarily resulting therefrom. They desire the existing state of society minus its revolutionary and disintegrating elements. They wish for a bourgeoisie without a proletariat. The bourgeoisie naturally conceives the world in which it is supreme to be the best; and bourgeois Socialism develops this comfortable conception into a more or less complete system. In requiring the proletariat to carry out such a system, and thereby to march straightway into the New Jerusalem, it but requires in reality, that the proletariat should remain within the bounds of existing society, but should cast away all its hateful ideas concerning the bourgeoisie.

A second and more practical, but less systematic, form of this Socialism sought to depreciate every revolutionary movement in the eyes of the working class, by showing that no mere political reform, but only a change in the material conditions of existence, in economical relations, could be of any advantage to them. By changes in the material conditions of existence, this form of Socialism, however, by no means understands abolition of the bourgeois relations of production, an abolition that can be effected only by a revolution, but administrative reforms, based on the continued existence of these relations; reforms, therefore, that in no respect affect the relations between capital and labour, but, at the best, lessen the cost, and simplify the administrative work, of bourgeois government.

Bourgeois Socialism attains adequate expression, when, and only when, it becomes a mere figure of speech.

Free trade: for the benefit of the working class. Protective duties: for the benefit of the working class. Solitary confinement: for the benefit of the working class. This is the last word and the only seriously meant word of bourgeois Socialism.

It is summed up in the phrase: the bourgeois is a bourgeois — for the benefit of the working class.

III. CRITICAL-UTOPIAN SOCIALISM AND COMMUNISM

We do not here refer to that literature which, in every great modern revolution, has always given voice to the demands of the proletariat, such as the writings of Babeuf and others.

The first direct attempts of the proletariat to attain its own ends, made in times of universal excitement, when feudal society was being overthrown, these attempts necessarily failed, owing to the then undeveloped state of the proletariat, as well as to the absence of the material conditions for its emancipation, conditions that had yet to be produced, and could be produced by the bourgeois epoch alone. The revolutionary literature that accompanied these first movements of the proletariat had necessarily a reactionary character. It inculcated universal asceticism and social levelling in its crudest form.

The Socialist and Communist systems properly so called, those of Saint-Simon, Fourier, Owen and others, spring into existence in the early undeveloped period, described above, of the struggle between proletariat and bourgeoisie (see Section I. Bourgeois and Proletarians).

The founders of these systems see, indeed, the class antagonisms, as well as the action of the decomposing elements in the prevailing form of society. But the proletariat offers to them the spectacle of a class without any historical initiative or any independent political movement.

Since the development of class antagonism keeps even pace with the development of industry, the economic situation, as they find it, does not as yet offer to them the material conditions for the emancipation of the proletariat. They therefore search after a new social science, after social laws, that are to create these conditions.

Social action is to yield to their personal inventive action, historically created conditions of emancipation to fantastic ones, and the gradual, class organization of the proletariat to an organization of society specially contrived by these inventors. Future history resolves itself, in their eyes, into the propaganda and the practical carrying out of their social plans.

In the formation of their plans they are conscious of caring chiefly for the interests of the working class, as being the most suffering class. Only from the point of view of being the most suffering class does the proletariat exist for them.

The undeveloped state of the class struggle, as well as their own surroundings, causes Socialists of this kind to consider themselves far superior to all class antagonisms. They want to improve the condition of every member of society, even that of the most favoured. Hence, they habitually appeal to society at large, without distinction of class; nay, by preference, to the ruling class. For how can people, when once they understand their system, fail to see in it the best possible plan of the best possible state of society?

Hence, they reject all political, and especially all revolutionary, action; they wish to attain their ends by peaceful means, and endeavour, by small experiments, necessarily doomed to failure, and by the force of example, to pave the way for the new social Gospel.

Such fantastic pictures of future society, painted at a time when the proletariat is still in a very undeveloped state and has but a fantastic conception of its own position correspond with the first instinctive yearnings of that class for a general reconstruction of society.

But these Socialist and Communist publications contain also a critical element. They attack every principle of existing society. Hence they are full of the most valuable materials for the enlightenment of the working class. Their positive propositions concerning the future society, for example, abolition of the contradiction between town and country, of the family, of private profit, of the wage system, the proclamation of social harmony, the conversion of the functions of the State into a mere superintendence of production, all these proposals point solely to the disappearance of class antagonisms which were, at that time, only just cropping up, and which, in these publications, are recognized in their earliest indistinct and undefined forms only. These proposals, therefore, are of a purely Utopian character.

The significance of Critical-Utopian Socialism and Communism bears an inverse relation to historical development. In proportion as the class struggle develops and takes definite shape, this fantastic standing apart from the contest, these fantastic attacks on it, lose all practical value and all theoretical justification. Therefore, although the originators of these systems were, in many respects, revolutionary, their disciples have, in every case, formed mere reactionary sects. They hold fast by the original views of their masters, in opposition to the progressive historical development of the proletariat. They, therefore, endeavour, and that consistently, to deaden the class struggle and to reconcile the class antagonisms. They still dream of experimental realization of their social Utopias, of founding isolated '*phalanstères*', of establishing 'Home Colonies', of setting up a 'Little Icaria'* – duodecimo editions of the New Jerusalem –

and to realize all these castles in the air, they are compelled to appeal to the feelings and purses of the bourgeois. By degrees they sink into the category of the reactionary conservative Socialists depicted above, differing from these only by more systematic pedantry, and by their fanatical and superstitious belief in the miraculous effects of their social science.

They, therefore, violently oppose all political action on the part of the working class; such action, according to them, can only result from blind unbelief in the new Gospel.

The Owenites in England, and the Fourierists in France, respectively oppose the Chartists and the *Réformistes*.

4

Position of the Communists in Relation to the Various Existing Opposition Parties

SECTION 2 has made clear the relations of the Communists to the existing working-class parties, such as the Chartists in England and the Agrarian Reformers in America.*

The Communists fight for the attainment of the immediate aims, for the enforcement of the momentary interests of the working class; but in the movement of the present, they also represent the future of that movement. In France the Communists ally themselves with the Social-Democrats,* against the conservative and radical bourgeoisie, reserving, however, the right to take up a critical position in regard to phrases and illusions traditionally handed down from the great Revolution.

In Switzerland they support the Radicals, without losing sight of the fact that this party consists of antagonistic elements, partly of Democratic Socialists, in the French sense, partly of radical bourgeois.

In Poland they support the party that insists on an agrarian revolution as the prime condition for national emancipation, that party which fomented the insurrection of Cracow in 1846.

In Germany they fight with the bourgeoisie whenever it acts in a revolutionary way, against the absolute monarchy, the feudal squirearchy, and the petty bourgeoisie.

But they never cease, for a single instant, to instil into the working class the clearest possible recognition of the hostile antagonism between bourgeoisie and proletariat, in order that the German workers may straightway use, as so many weapons against the bourgeoisie, the social and political conditions that the bourgeoisie must necessarily introduce along with its supremacy, and in order that, after the fall of the reactionary classes in Germany, the fight against the bourgeoisie itself may immediately begin.

The Communists turn their attention chiefly to Germany, because that country is on the eve of a bourgeois revolution that is bound to be carried out under more advanced conditions of European civilization, and with a much more developed proletariat, than that of England was in the seventeenth, and of France in the eighteenth century, and because the bourgeois revolution in Germany will be but the prelude to an immediately following proletarian revolution.

In short, the Communists everywhere support every revolutionary movement against the existing social and political order of things.

In all these movements they bring to the front, as the leading question in each, the property question, no matter what its degree of development at the time.

Finally, they labour everywhere for the union and agreement of the democratic parties of all countries.

The Communists disdain to conceal their views and aims. They openly declare that their ends can be attained only by the forcible overthrow of all existing social conditions. Let the ruling classes tremble at a Communistic revolution. The proletarians have nothing to lose but their chains. They have a world to win.

WORKING MEN OF ALL COUNTRIES, UNITE!

Preface to the German Edition of 1872

THE Communist League, an international association of workers, which could of course be only a secret one under the conditions obtaining at the time, commissioned the undersigned, at the Congress held in London in November, 1847, to draw up for publication a detailed theoretical and practical programme of the Party. Such was the origin of the following Manifesto, the manuscript of which travelled to London, to be printed, a few weeks before the February Revolution.* First published in German, it has been republished in that language in at least twelve different editions in Germany, England and America. It was published in English for the first time in 1850 in the *Red Republican*,* London, translated by Miss Helen Macfarlane, and in 1871 in at least three different translations in America. A French version first appeared in Paris shortly before the June insurrection of 1848* and recently in *Le Socialiste* of New York.* A new translation is in the course of preparation. A Polish version appeared in London shortly after it was first published in German. A Russian translation was published in Geneva in the sixties. Into Danish, too, it was translated shortly after its first appearance.

However much the state of things may have altered during the last twenty-five years, the general principles laid down in this Manifesto are, on the whole, as correct today as ever. Here and there some detail might be improved. The practical application of the principles will depend, as the Manifesto itself states, everywhere and at all times, on the historical conditions for the time being existing, and, for that reason, no special stress is laid on the revolutionary measures proposed at the end of Section II. That passage would, in many respects, be very differently worded today. In view of the gigantic strides of Modern Industry in the last twenty-five years, and of the accompanying improved and extended party organization of the working class, in view of the practical experience gained, first in the February Revolution, and then, still more, in the Paris Commune,* where the proletariat for the first time held political power for two whole months, this programme has in some details become antiquated. One thing especially was proved by the Commune, viz., that 'the working class cannot simply lay hold of the ready-made State machinery, and wield it for its own purposes'. (See *The Civil War in France; Address of the General Council of the International Working Men's Association*, London, Truelove, 1871, p. 15, where this point is further developed.*) Further, it is self-evident that the criticism of Socialist literature is deficient in relation to the present time, because it comes down only to 1847; also that the remarks on the relation of the Communists to the various opposition parties (Section IV), although in principle still correct, yet in practice are antiquated, because the political situation has been entirely changed, and the progress of history has swept from off the earth the greater portion of the political parties there enumerated.

But, then, the Manifesto has become a historical document which we have no longer any right to alter. A subsequent edition may perhaps appear with an introduction bridging the gap from 1847 to the present day; this reprint was too unexpected to leave us time for that.

London, 24 June 1872   KARL MARX
                                     FREDERICK ENGELS

Preface to the Russian Edition of 1882

THE first Russian edition of the *Manifesto of the Communist Party*, translated by Bakunin, was published early in the sixties by the printing office of the *Kolokol*.* Then the West could see in it (the *Russian* edition of the Manifesto) only a literary curiosity. Such a view would be impossible today.

What a limited field the proletarian movement still occupied at that time (December 1847) is most clearly shown by the last section of the Manifesto: the position of the Communists in relation to the various opposition parties in the various countries. Precisely Russia and the United States are missing here. It was the time when Russia constituted the last great reserve of all European reaction, when the United States absorbed the surplus proletarian forces of Europe through immigration. Both countries provided Europe with raw materials and were at the same time markets for the sale of its industrial products. At that time both were, therefore, in one way or another, pillars of the existing European order.

How very different today! Precisely European immigration fitted North America for a gigantic agricultural production, whose competition is shaking the very foundations of European landed property – large and small. In addition it enabled the United States to exploit its tremendous industrial resources with an energy and on a scale that must shortly break the industrial monopoly of Western Europe, and especially of England, existing up to now. Both circumstances react in revolutionary manner upon America itself. Step by step the small and middle landownership of the farmers, the basis of the whole political constitution, is succumbing to the competition of giant farms; simultaneously, a mass proletariat and a fabulous concentration of capitals are developing for the first time in the industrial regions.

And now Russia! During the Revolution of 1848–49 not only the European princes, but the European bourgeois as well, found their only salvation from the proletariat, just beginning to awaken, in Russian intervention. The tsar was proclaimed the chief of European reaction. Today he is a prisoner of war of the revolution, in Gatchina,* and Russia forms the vanguard of revolutionary action in Europe.

The Communist Manifesto had as its object the proclamation of the inevitably impending dissolution of modern bourgeois property. But in Russia we find, face to face with the rapidly developing capitalist swindle and bourgeois landed property, just beginning to develop, more than half the land owned in common by the peasants. Now the question is: can the Russian *obshchina*,* though greatly undermined, yet a form of the primeval common ownership of land, pass directly to the higher form of communist common ownership? Or on the contrary, must it first pass through the same process of dissolution as constitutes the historical evolution of the West?

The only answer to that possible today is this: If the Russian Revolution becomes the signal for a proletarian revolution in the West, so that both complement each other, the present Russian common ownership of land may serve as the starting point for a communist development.

London, 21 January 1882   KARL MARX
                                 FREDERICK ENGELS

Preface to the German Edition of 1883

THE preface to the present edition I must, alas, sign alone. Marx – the man to whom the whole working class of Europe and America owes more than to anyone else – rests at Highgate Cemetery and over his grave the first grass is already growing. Since his death, there can be even less thought of revising or supplementing the Manifesto. All the more do I consider it necessary again to state here the following expressly:

The basic thought running through the Manifesto – that economic production and the structure of society of every historical epoch necessarily arising therefrom constitute the foundation for the political and intellectual history of that epoch; that consequently (ever since the dissolution of the primeval communal ownership of land) all history has been a history of class struggles, of struggles between exploited and exploiting, between dominated and dominating classes at various stages of social development; that this struggle, however, has now reached a stage where the exploited and oppressed class (the proletariat) can no longer emancipate itself from the class which exploits and oppresses it (the bourgeoisie), without at the same time for ever freeing the whole of society from exploitation, oppression and class struggles – this basic thought belongs solely and exclusively to Marx.*

I have already stated this many times; but precisely now it is necessary that it also stand in front of the Manifesto itself.

London, 28 June 1883   F. ENGELS

Preface to the English Edition of 1888

THE Manifesto was published as the platform of the 'Communist League', a working men's association, first exclusively German, later on international, and, under the political conditions of the Continent before 1848, unavoidably a secret society. At a Congress of the League, held in London in November, 1847, Marx and Engels were commissioned to prepare for publication a complete theoretical and practical party programme. Drawn up in German, in January, 1848, the manuscript was sent to the printer in London a few weeks before the French revolution of February 24th. A French translation was brought out in Paris, shortly before the insurrection of June, 1848. The first English translation, by Miss Helen Macfarlane, appeared in George Julian Harney's *Red Republican*, London, 1850. A Danish and a Polish edition had also been published.

The defeat of the Parisian insurrection of June, 1848 – the first great battle between Proletariat and Bourgeoisie – drove again into the background, for a time, the social and political aspirations of the European working class. Thenceforth, the struggle for supremacy was again, as it had been before the revolution of February, solely between different sections of the propertied class; the working class was reduced to a fight for political elbow-room, and to the position of extreme wing of the middle-class Radicals. Wherever independent proletarian movements continued to show signs of life, they were ruthlessly hunted down. Thus the Prussian police hunted out the Central Board of the Communist League, then located in Cologne. The members were arrested, and, after eighteen months' imprisonment, they were tried in October, 1852. This celebrated 'Cologne Communist trial' lasted from October 4th till November 12th; seven of the prisoners were sentenced to terms of imprisonment in a fortress, varying from three to six years. Immediately after the sentence, the League was formally dissolved by the remaining members. As to the Manifesto, it seemed thenceforth to be doomed to oblivion.

When the European working class had recovered sufficient strength for another attack on the ruling classes, the International Working Men's Association sprang up. But this association, formed with the express aim of welding into one body the whole militant proletariat of Europe and America, could not at once proclaim the principles laid down in the Manifesto. The International was bound to have a programme broad enough to be acceptable to the English Trades Unions, to the followers of Proudhon in France, Belgium, Italy, and Spain, and to the Lassalleans* in Germany. Marx who drew up this programme to the satisfaction of all parties, entirely trusted to the intellectual development of the working class, which was sure to result from combined action and mutual discussion. The very events and vicissitudes of the struggle against Capital, the defeats even more than the victories, could not help bringing home to men's minds the insufficiency of their various favourite nostrums, and preparing the way for a more complete insight into the true conditions of working-class emancipation. And Marx was right. The International, on its breaking up in 1874, left the workers quite different men from what it had found them in 1864. Proudhonism in France, Lassalleanism in Germany were dying out, and even the conservative English Trades Unions, though most of them had long since severed their connexion with the International, were gradually advancing towards that point at which, last year at Swansea, their President could say in their name 'Continental Socialism has lost its terrors for us'. In fact: the principles of the Manifesto had made considerable headway among the working men of all countries.

The Manifesto itself thus came to the front again. The German text had been, since 1850, reprinted several times in Switzerland, England and America. In 1872, it was translated into

English in New York, where the translation was published in *Woodhull and Claflin's Weekly*. From this English version, a French one was made in *Le Socialiste* of New York. Since then at least two more English translations, more or less mutilated, have been brought out in America, and one of them has been reprinted in England. The first Russian translation, made by Bakunin, was published at Herzen's *Kolokol* office in Geneva, about 1863;* a second one, by the heroic Vera Zasulich, also in Geneva, 1882. A new Danish edition is to be found in *Social-demokratisk Bibliothek*, Copenhagen, 1885; a fresh French translation in *Le Socialiste*, Paris 1885. From this latter a Spanish version was prepared and published in Madrid, 1886. The German reprints are not to be counted, there have been twelve altogether at the least. An Armenian translation, which was to be published in Constantinople some months ago, did not see the light, I am told, because the publisher was afraid of bringing out a book with the name of Marx on it, while the translator declined to call it his own production. Of further translations into other languages I have heard, but have not seen them. Thus the history of the Manifesto reflects, to a great extent, the history of the modern working-class movement; at present it is undoubtedly the most widespread, the most international production of all Socialist literature, the common platform acknowledged by millions of working men from Siberia to California.

Yet, when it was written, we could not have called it a *Socialist* Manifesto. By Socialists, in 1847, were understood, on the one hand, the adherents of the various Utopian systems: Owenites in England, Fourierists in France, both of them already reduced to the position of mere sects, and gradually dying out; on the other hand, the most multifarious social quacks, who, by all manners of tinkering, professed to redress, without any danger to capital and profit, all sorts of social grievances; in both cases men outside the working-class movement, and looking rather to the 'educated' classes for support. Whatever portion of the working class had become convinced of the insufficiency of mere political revolutions, and had proclaimed the necessity of a total social change, that portion then called itself Communist. It was a crude, rough-hewn, purely instinctive sort of Communism; still, it touched the cardinal point and was powerful enough amongst the working class to produce the Utopian Communism, in France, of Cabet, and in Germany, of Weitling. Thus, Socialism was, in 1847, a middle-class movement, Communism, a working-class movement. Socialism was, on the Continent at least, 'respectable'; Communism was the very opposite. And as our notion, from the very beginning, was that 'the emancipation of the working class must be the act of the working class itself', there could be no doubt as to which of the two names we must take. Moreover, we have, ever since, been far from repudiating it.

The Manifesto being our joint production, I consider myself bound to state that the fundamental proposition, which forms its nucleus, belongs to Marx. That proposition is: that in every historical epoch, the prevailing mode of economic production and exchange, and the social organization necessarily following from it, form the basis upon which is built up, and from which alone can be explained, the political and intellectual history of that epoch; that subsequently the whole history of mankind (since the dissolution of primitive tribal society, holding land in common ownership) has been a history of class struggles, contests between exploiting and exploited, ruling and oppressed classes; that the history of these class struggles forms a series of evolutions in which, nowadays, a stage has been reached where the exploited and oppressed class – the proletariat – cannot attain its emancipation from the sway of the exploiting and ruling class – the bourgeoisie – without, at the same time, and once and for all, emancipating society at large from all exploitation, oppression, class distinctions and class struggles.

This proposition which, in my opinion, is destined to do for history what Darwin's theory has done for biology, we, both of us, had been gradually approaching for some years before 1845. How far I had independently progressed towards it, is best shown by my *Condition of the Working Class in England.** But when I again met Marx at Brussels, in spring, 1845, he had it ready worked out, and put it before me, in terms almost as clear as those in which I have stated it here.

From our joint preface to the German edition of 1872, I quote the following:

'However much the state of things may have altered during the last twenty-five years, the general principles laid down in this Manifesto are, on the whole, as correct today as ever. Here and there some detail might be improved. The practical application of the principles will depend, as the Manifesto itself states, everywhere and at all times, on the historical conditions for the time being existing, and, for that reason, no special stress is laid on the revolutionary measures proposed at the end of Section II. That passage would, in many respects, be very differently worded today. In view of the gigantic strides of Modern Industry since 1848, and of the accompanying improved and extended organization of the working class, in view of the practical experience gained, first in the February Revolution, and then, still more, in the Paris Commune, where the proletariat for the first time held political power for two whole months, this programme has in some details become antiquated. One thing especially was proved by the Commune, viz., that "the working class cannot simply lay hold of the ready-made State machinery, and wield it for its own purposes". (See *The Civil War in France; Address of the General Council of the International Working Men's Association*, London, Truelove, 1871, p. 15, where this point is further developed.) Further, it is self-evident that the criticism of Socialist literature is deficient in relation to the present time, because it comes down only to 1847; also, that the remarks on the relation of the Communists to the various opposition parties (Section IV), although in principle still correct, yet in practice are antiquated, because the political situation has been entirely changed, and the progress of history has swept off the earth the greater portion of the political parties there enumerated.

'But then, the Manifesto has become a historical document which we have no longer any right to alter.'

The present translation is by Mr Samuel Moore, the translator of the greater portion of Marx's *Capital*. We have revised it in common, and I have added a few notes explanatory of historical allusions.

London, 30 January 1888   F. ENGELS

Preface to the German Edition of 1890

SINCE the above was written,* a new German edition of the Manifesto has again become necessary, and much has also happened to the Manifesto which should be recorded here.

A second Russian translation – by Vera Zasulich – appeared at Geneva in 1882; the preface to that edition was written by Marx and myself. Unfortunately, the original German manuscript has gone astray; I must therefore retranslate from the Russian, which will in no way improve the text. It reads:

'The first Russian edition of the *Manifesto of the Communist Party*, translated by Bakunin, was published early in the sixties by the printing office of the *Kolokol*. Then the West could see in it (the Russian edition of the Manifesto) only a literary curiosity. Such a view would be impossible today.

'What a limited field the proletarian movement still occupied at that time (December 1847) is most clearly shown by the last section of the Manifesto: the position of the Communists in relation to the various opposition parties in the various countries. Precisely Russia and the United States are missing here. It was the time when Russia constituted the last great reserve of all European reaction, when the United States absorbed the surplus proletarian forces of Europe through immigration. Both countries provided Europe with raw materials and were at the same time markets for the sale of its industrial products. At that time both were, therefore, in one way or another, pillars of the existing European order.

'How very different today! Precisely European immigration fitted North America for a gigantic agricultural production, whose competition is shaking the very foundations of European landed property – large and small. In addition it enabled the United States to exploit its tremendous industrial resources with an energy and on a scale that must shortly break the industrial monopoly of Western Europe, and especially of England, existing up to now. Both circumstances react in revolutionary manner upon America itself. Step by step the small and middle landownership of the farmers, the basis of the whole political constitution, is succumbing to the competition of giant farms; simultaneously, a mass proletariat and a fabulous concentration of capitals are developing for the first time in the industrial regions.

'And now Russia! During the Revolution of 1848–49 not only the European princes, but the European bourgeois as well, found their only salvation from the proletariat, just beginning to awaken, in Russian intervention. The tsar was proclaimed the chief of European reaction. Today he is a prisoner of war of the revolution, in Gatchina, and Russia forms the vanguard of revolutionary action in Europe.

'The Communist Manifesto had as its object the proclamation of the inevitably impending dissolution of modern bourgeois property. But in Russia we find, face to face with the rapidly developing capitalist swindle and bourgeois landed property, just beginning to develop, more than half the land owned in common by the peasants. Now the question is: can the Russian *obshchina*, though greatly undermined, yet a form of the primeval common ownership of land, pass directly to the higher form of communist common ownership? Or on the contrary, must it first pass through the same process of dissolution as constitutes the historical evolution of the West?

'The only answer to that possible today is this: If the Russian Revolution becomes the signal for a proletarian revolution in the West, so that both complement each other, the present Russian common ownership of land may serve as the starting point for a communist development.

'*London, 21 January 1882*   KARL MARX
                                    FREDERICK ENGELS'

At about the same date, a new Polish version appeared in Geneva: *Manifest Komunistyczny*.

Furthermore, a new Danish translation has appeared in the *Social-demokratisk Bibliothek*, Copenhagen, 1885. Unfortunately it is not quite complete; certain essential passages, which seem to have presented difficulties to the translator, have been omitted, and in addition there are signs of carelessness here and there, which are all the more unpleasantly conspicuous since the translation indicates that had the translator taken a little more pains he would have done an excellent piece of work.

A new French version appeared in 1885 in *Le Socialiste* of Paris; it is the best published to date.

From this latter a Spanish version was published the same year, first in *El Socialista* of Madrid, and then reissued in pamphlet form: *Manifesto del Partido Comunista* por Carlos Marx y F. Engels, Madrid, Administración de *El Socialista*, Hernán Cortés 8.

As a matter of curiosity I may also mention that in 1887 the manuscript of an Armenian translation was offered to a publisher in Constantinople. But the good man did not have the courage to publish something bearing the name of Marx and suggested that the translator set down his own name as author, which the latter, however, declined.

After one and then another of the more or less inaccurate American translations had been repeatedly reprinted in England, an authentic version at last appeared in 1888. This was by my friend Samuel Moore, and we went through it together once more before it was sent to press. It is entitled: *Manifesto of the Communist Party*, by Karl Marx and Frederick Engels. Authorized English Translation, edited and annotated by Frederick Engels, 1888. London, William Reeves, 185 Fleet st., E.C. I have added some of the notes of that edition to the present one.

The Manifesto has had a history of its own. Greeted with enthusiasm, at the time of its appearance, by the then still not at all numerous vanguard of scientific Socialism (as is proved by the translations mentioned in the first preface), it was soon forced into the background by the reaction that began with the defeat of the Paris workers in June 1848, and was finally excommunicated 'according to law' by the conviction of the Cologne Communists in November 1852. With the disappearance from the public scene of the workers' movement that had begun with the February Revolution, the Manifesto too passed into the background.

When the working class of Europe had again gathered sufficient strength for a new onslaught upon the power of the ruling classes, the International Working Men's Association came into being. Its aim was to weld together into *one* huge army the whole militant working class of Europe and America. Therefore it could not *set out* from the principles laid down in the Manifesto. It was bound to have a programme which would not shut the door on the English trade unions, the French, Belgian, Italian and Spanish Proudhonists and the German Lassalleans. This programme – the preamble to the Rules of the International – was drawn up by Marx* with a master hand acknowledged even by Bakunin and the Anarchists. For the ultimate triumph of the ideas set forth in the Manifesto Marx relied solely and exclusively upon the intellectual development of the working class, as it necessarily had to ensue from united action and discussion. The events and vicissitudes in the struggle against capital, the defeats even more than the successes, could not but demonstrate to the fighters the inadequacy hitherto of their universal panaceas and make their minds more receptive to a thorough understanding of the true conditions for the emancipation of the workers. And Marx was right. The working class of 1874, at the dissolution of the International, was altogether different from that of 1864, at its foundation. Proudhonism in the Latin countries and the specific Lassalleanism in Germany were dying out, and even the then arch-conservative English trade unions were gradually approaching the point where in 1887 the chairman of their Swansea Congress could say in their name 'Continental Socialism has lost its terrors for us'. Yet by 1887 Continental

Socialism was almost exclusively the theory heralded in the Manifesto. Thus, to a certain extent, the history of the Manifesto reflects the history of the modern working-class movement since 1848. At present it is doubtless the most widely circulated, the most international product of all Socialist literature, the common programme of many millions of workers of all countries, from Siberia to California.

Nevertheless, when it appeared we could not have called it a *Socialist* Manifesto. In 1847 two kinds of people were considered Socialists. On the one hand were the adherents of the various Utopian systems, notably the Owenites in England and the Fourierists in France, both of whom at that date had already dwindled to mere sects gradually dying out. On the other, the manifold types of social quacks who wanted to eliminate social abuses through their various universal panaceas and all kinds of patchwork, without hurting capital and profit in the least. In both cases, people who stood outside the labour movement and who looked for support rather to the 'educated' classes. The section of the working class, however, which demanded a radical reconstruction of society, convinced that mere political revolutions were not enough, then called itself *Communist*. It was still a rough-hewn, only instinctive, and frequently somewhat crude Communism. Yet it was powerful enough to bring into being two systems of Utopian Communism – in France the 'Icarian' Communism of Cabet, and in Germany that of Weitling. Socialism in 1847 signified a bourgeois movement, Communism, a working-class movement. Socialism was, on the Continent at least, quite respectable, whereas Communism was the very opposite. And since we were very decidedly of the opinion as early as then that 'the emancipation of the workers must be the act of the working class itself', we could have no hesitation as to which of the two names we should choose. Nor has it ever occurred to us since to repudiate it.

'Working men of all countries, unite!' But few voices responded when we proclaimed these words to the world forty-two years ago, on the eve of the first Paris Revolution in which the proletariat came out with demands of its own. On 28 September 1864, however, the proletarians of most of the Western European countries joined hands in the International Working Men's Association of glorious memory. True, the International itself lived only nine years. But that the eternal union of the proletarians of all countries created by it is still alive and lives stronger than ever, there is no better witness than this day. Because today, as I write these lines, the European and American proletariat is reviewing its fighting forces, mobilised for the first time, mobilised as *one* army, under *one* flag, for *one* immediate aim: the standard eight-hour working day, to be established by legal enactment, as proclaimed by the Geneva Congress of the International in 1866, and again by the Paris Workers' Congress in 1889.* And today's spectacle will open the eyes of the capitalists and landlords of all countries to the fact that today the working men of all countries are united indeed.

If only Marx were still by my side to see this with his own eyes!

London, 1 May 1890   F. ENGELS

Preface to the Polish Edition of 1892

THE fact that a new Polish edition of the Communist Manifesto has become necessary gives rise to various thoughts.

First of all, it is noteworthy that of late the Manifesto has become an index, as it were, on the development of large-scale industry on the European continent. In proportion as large-scale industry expands in a given country, the demand grows among the workers of that country for enlightenment regarding their position as the working class in relation to the possessing classes, the socialist movement spreads among them and the demand for the Manifesto increases. Thus, not only the state of the labour movement but also the degree of development of large-scale industry can be measured with fair accuracy in every country by the number of copies of the Manifesto circulated in the language of that country.

Accordingly, the new Polish edition indicates a decided progress of Polish industry. And there can be no doubt whatever that this progress since the previous edition published ten years ago has actually taken place. Russian Poland, Congress Poland, has become the big industrial region of the Russian Empire. Whereas Russian large-scale industry is scattered sporadically – a part round the Gulf of Finland, another in the centre (Moscow and Vladimir), a third along the coasts of the Black and Azov seas, and still others elsewhere – Polish industry has been packed into a relatively small area and enjoys both the advantages and the disadvantages arising from such concentration. The competing Russian manufacturers acknowledged the advantages when they demanded protective tariffs against Poland, in spite of their ardent desire to transform the Poles into Russians. The disadvantages – for the Polish manufacturers and the Russian government – are manifest in the rapid spread of socialist ideas among the Polish workers and in the growing demand for the Manifesto.

But the rapid development of Polish industry, outstripping that of Russia, is in its turn a new proof of the inexhaustible vitality of the Polish people and a new guarantee of its impending national restoration. And the restoration of an independent strong Poland is a matter which concerns not only the Poles but all of us. A sincere international collaboration of the European nations is possible only if each of these nations is fully autonomous in its own house. The Revolution of 1848, which under the banner of the proletariat, after all, merely let the proletarian fighters do the work of the bourgeoisie, also secured the independence of Italy, Germany, and Hungary through its testamentary executors, Louis Bonaparte and Bismarck; but Poland, which since 1792 had done more for the Revolution than all these three together, was left to its own resources when it succumbed in 1863 to a tenfold greater Russian force. The nobility could neither maintain nor regain Polish independence; today, to the bourgeoisie, this independence is, to say the least, immaterial. Nevertheless, it is a necessity for the harmonious collaboration of the European nations. It can be gained only by the young Polish proletariat, and in its hands it is secure. For the workers of all the rest of Europe need the independence of Poland just as much as the Polish workers themselves.

London, 10 February 1892   F. ENGELS

Preface to the Italian Edition of 1893

TO THE ITALIAN READER

PUBLICATION of the *Manifesto of the Communist Party* co-
incided, one may say, with 18 March 1848, the day of the revolutions in Milan and Berlin, which were armed uprisings of the
two nations situated in the centre, the one, of the continent of
Europe, the other, of the Mediterranean; two nations until then
enfeebled by division and internal strife, and thus fallen under
foreign domination. While Italy was subject to the Emperor of
Austria, Germany underwent the yoke, not less effective though
more indirect, of the Tsar of all the Russias. The consequences
of 18 March 1848 freed both Italy and Germany from this dis-
grace; if from 1848 to 1871 these two great nations were
reconstituted and somehow again put on their own, it was, as
Karl Marx used to say, because the men who suppressed the
Revolution of 1848 were, nevertheless, its testamentary
executors in spite of themselves.

Everywhere that revolution was the work of the working
class; it was the latter that built the barricades and paid with its
lifeblood. Only the Paris workers, in overthrowing the government, had the very definite intention of overthrowing the bourgeois regime. But conscious though they were of the fatal
antagonism existing between their own class and the bourgeoisie, still, neither the economic progress of the country nor
the intellectual development of the mass of French workers had
as yet reached the stage which would have made a social reconstruction possible. In the final analysis, therefore, the fruits of
the revolution were reaped by the capitalist class. In the other
countries, in Italy, in Germany, in Austria, the workers, from the

very outset, did nothing but raise the bourgeoisie to power. But in any country the rule of the bourgeoisie is impossible without national independence. Therefore, the Revolution of 1848 had to bring in its train the unity and autonomy of the nations that had lacked them up to then: Italy, Germany, Hungary, Poland will follow in turn.

Thus, if the Revolution of 1848 was not a socialist revolution, it paved the way, prepared the ground for the latter. Through the impetus given to large-scale industry in all countries, the bourgeois regime during the last forty-five years has everywhere created a numerous, concentrated and powerful proletariat. It has thus raised, to use the language of the Manifesto, its own gravediggers. Without restoring autonomy and unity to each nation, it will be impossible to achieve the international union of the proletariat, or the peaceful and intelligent cooperation of these nations towards common aims. Just imagine joint international action by the Italian, Hungarian, German, Polish and Russian workers under the political conditions preceding 1848!

The battles fought in 1848 were thus not fought in vain. Nor have the forty-five years separating us from that revolutionary epoch passed to no purpose. The fruits are ripening, and all I wish is that the publication of this Italian translation may augur as well for the victory of the Italian proletariat as the publication of the original did for the international revolution.

The Manifesto does full justice to the revolutionary part played by capitalism in the past. The first capitalist nation was Italy. The close of the feudal Middle Ages, and the opening of the modern capitalist era are marked by a colossal figure: an Italian, Dante, both the last poet of the Middle Ages and the first poet of modern times. Today, as in 1300, a new historical era is approaching. Will Italy give us the new Dante, who will mark the hour of birth of this new, proletarian era?

London, 1 February 1893   F. ENGELS

EXPLANATORY NOTES

All notes are by the Editor, except for those by Engels, which are indicated by square brackets at the end of the note.

3 *Bourgeois and Proletarians*: by bourgeoisie is meant the class of modern Capitalists, owners of the means of social production and employers of wage labour. By proletariat, the class of modern wage-labourers who, having no means of production of their own, are reduced to selling their labour power in order to live. [Note by Engels to the English edition of 1888.]

The history of all hitherto existing society: that is, all *written* history. In 1847, the pre-history of society, the social organization existing previous to recorded history, was all but unknown. Since then, Haxthausen discovered common ownership of land in Russia, Maurer proved it to be the social foundation from which all Teutonic races started in history, and by and by village communities were found to be, or to have been the primitive form of society everywhere from India to Ireland. The inner organization of this primitive Communistic society was laid bare, in its typical form, by Morgan's crowning discovery of the true nature of the *gens* and its relation to the *tribe*. With the dissolution of these primeval communities society begins to be differentiated into separate and finally antagonistic classes. I have attempted to retrace this process of dissolution in: *Der Ursprung der Familie, des Privateigenthums und des Staats* (the Origin of the Family, Private Property and the State), 2nd edition, Stuttgart 1886. [Note by Engels to the English edition of 1888.]

Guild-master: that is, a full member of a guild, a master within, not a head of a guild. [Note by Engels to the English edition of 1888.]

4 *the medieval commune*: 'Commune' was the name taken, in France, by the nascent towns even before they had conquered from their feudal lords and masters local self-government and

political rights as the 'Third Estate'. Generally speaking, for the
economical development of the bourgeoisie, England is here
taken as the typical country; for its political development, France.
[Note by Engels to the English edition of 1888.]

This was the name given their urban communities by the
townsmen of Italy and France, after they had purchased or
wrested their initial rights of self-government from their feudal
lords. [Note by Engels to the German edition of 1890.]

12 *the Ten Hours bill . . . was carried:* limiting the working-day for
women and children to ten hours, passed in 1847.

27 *the French revolution . . . English reform agitation:* in 1830 a revolution replaced the Bourbon Charles X by the so-called 'bourgeois'
monarch Louis-Philippe. In 1832 in Britain the First Reform Bill
gave the vote to the heads of substantial households.

the restoration period: not the English Restoration 1660 to 1689,
but the French Restoration 1814 to 1830. [Note by Engels to the
English edition of 1888.]

28 *French Legitimists and 'Young England':* the Legitimists were
a party of aristocratic landowners who wished to see the
restoration, yet again, of the Bourbon dynasty. 'Young England'
was a group of Tory writers and politicians, including Disraeli
and Carlyle, founded in 1841, who advocated a regenerated
feudalism.

to barter truth . . . potato spirits: this applies chiefly to Germany
where the landed aristocracy and squirearchy have large portions
of their estates cultivated for their own account by stewards, and
are, moreover, extensive beetroot-sugar manufacturers and dis-
tillers of potato spirits. The wealthier British aristocracy are, as
yet, rather above that; but they, too, know how to make up for
declining rents by lending their names to floaters of more or less
shady joint-stock companies. [Note by Engels to the English
edition of 1888.]

30 *the demands of 'Practical Reason':* allusion to Kant's *Critique of
Practical Reason*, published in 1788.

33 *foul and enervating literature:* the revolutionary storm of 1848
swept away this whole shabby tendency and cured its protagonists
of the desire to dabble further in Socialism. The chief

representative and classical type of this tendency is Herr Karl Grun. [Note by Engels to the German edition of 1890.]

33 *Proudhon's Philosophie de la Misère ... of this form*: Marx had subjected Proudhon's *Philosophy of Poverty* to devastating criticism in his *Poverty of Philosophy*, published in 1847.

36 *'phalanstères' ... 'Little Icaria'*: *Phalanstères* were Socialist colonies on the plan of Charles Fourier; *Icaria* was the name given by Cabet to his Utopia and, later on, to his American Communist colony. [Note by Engels to the English edition of 1888.]

'Home colonies' were what Owen called his Communist model societies. *Phalanstères* was the name of the public palaces planned by Fourier. *Icaria* was the name given to the Utopian land of fancy, whose Communist institutions Cabet portrayed. [Note by Engels to the German edition of 1890.]

38 *Agrarian Reformers in America*: the Agrarian (or National) Reform Association, founded in 1845, which advocated a free plot of land for every citizen.

Social-Democrats: the party then represented in Parliament by Ledru-Rollin, in literature by Louis Blanc, in the daily press by the *Réforme*. The name of Social-Democracy signified, with these its inventors, a section of the Democratic or Republican party more or less tinged with Socialism. [Note by Engels to the English edition of 1888.]

The party in France which at that time called itself Socialist-Democratic was represented in political life by Ledru-Rollin and in literature by Louis Blanc; thus it differed immeasurably from present-day German Social-Democracy. [Note by Engels to the German edition of 1890.]

40 *the February Revolution*: of 1848 in France, which overturned the 'bourgeois' monarchy of Louis-Philippe.

Red Republican: a short-lived Chartist newspaper published by Julian Harney.

the June insurrection of 1848: an insurrection provoked by the closing of the National Workshops. It was crushed by General Cavaignac.

40 *Le Socialiste of New York*: a publication of the French section of the First International in the United States.

41 *the Paris Commune*: of April and May of 1871, a socialist-inspired revolt of the people of Paris in the aftermath of the French defeat in the Franco-Prussian War.

The Civil War in France ... further developed: see Karl Marx, *Selected Writings*, ed. D. McLellan (Oxford, 1977), 539 ff.

42 *published early in the sixties ... Kolokol*: in fact, this edition appeared in 1869. It formed the basis for the 1882 edition which was revised by Plekhanov.

43 *in Gatchina*: after the assassination of Alexander II by social revolutionaries in 1881, his son Alexander III retired, for security reasons, to his palace at Gatchina near St Petersburg.

obshchina: village community.

44 *solely and exclusively to Marx*: 'This proposition', I wrote in the preface to the English translation, 'which in my opinion, is destined to do for history what Darwin's theory has done for biology, we, both of us, had been gradually approaching for some years before 1845. How far I had independently progressed towards it, is best shown by my *Condition of the Working Class in England*. But when I again met Marx at Brussels, in spring, 1845, he had it ready worked out, and put it before me, in terms almost as clear as those in which I have stated it here.' [Note by Engels to the German edition of 1890.]

46 *the Lassalleans*: Lassalle personally, to us, always acknowledged himself to be a disciple of Marx, and, as such, stood on the ground of the Manifesto. But in his public agitation, 1862–4, he did not go beyond demanding co-operative workshops supported by state credit. [Note by Engels.]

47 *by Bakunin ... about 1863*: Engels makes two mistakes here – see note to p. 42 above.

48 *Condition of the Working Class in England*: *The Condition of the Working Class in England in 1844*. By Frederick Engels. Translated by Florence K. Wischnewetzky, New York. Lovell – London. W. Reeves, 1888. [Note by Engels.]

51 *Since the above was written*:   Engels is referring to his preface to the German edition of 1883.

54 *drawn up by Marx*:   see Karl Marx and Friedrich Engels, *Selected Works* (Moscow, 1962), i. 386 ff.

56 *the Paris Workers' Congress in 1889*:   this was the Congress which inaugurated the Second International.

INDEX OF NAMES

Bhagavad Gita

The Bible Authorized King James Version
  With Apocrypha

Dhammapada

Dharmasūtras

The Koran

The Pañcatantra

The Sauptikaparvan (from the
  Mahabharata)

The Tale of Sinuhe and Other Ancient
  Egyptian Poems

Upaniṣads

ANSELM OF CANTERBURY   The Major Works

THOMAS AQUINAS   Selected Philosophical Writings

AUGUSTINE   The Confessions
  On Christian Teaching

BEDE   The Ecclesiastical History

HEMACANDRA   The Lives of the Jain Elders

KĀLIDĀSA   The Recognition of Śakuntalā

MANJHAN   Madhumalati

ŚĀNTIDEVA   The Bodhicaryāvatāra

The Oxford World's Classics Website

www.worldsclassics.co.uk

- Information about new titles
- Explore the full range of Oxford World's Classics
- Links to other literary sites and the main OUP webpage
- Imaginative competitions, with bookish prizes
- Peruse the Oxford World's Classics Magazine
- Articles by editors
- Extracts from Introductions
- A forum for discussion and feedback on the series
- Special information for teachers and lecturers

www.worldsclassics.co.uk

American Literature

British and Irish Literature

Children's Literature

Classics and Ancient Literature

Colonial Literature

Eastern Literature

European Literature

History

Medieval Literature

Oxford English Drama

Poetry

Philosophy

Politics

Religion

The Oxford Shakespeare

A complete list of Oxford Paperbacks, including Oxford World's Classics, Oxford Shakespeare, Oxford Drama, and Oxford Paperback Reference, is available in the UK from the Academic Division Publicity Department, Oxford University Press, Great Clarendon Street, Oxford OX2 6DP.

In the USA, complete lists are available from the Paperbacks Marketing Manager, Oxford University Press, 198 Madison Avenue, New York, NY 10016.

Oxford Paperbacks are available from all good bookshops. In case of difficulty, customers in the UK can order direct from Oxford University Press Bookshop, Freepost, 116 High Street, Oxford OX1 4BR, enclosing full payment. Please add 10 per cent of published price for postage and packing.